EARTH BELOW,
HEAVEN ABOVE

EARTH BELOW, HEAVEN ABOVE

a Portrait of India

CAROLYN NORTH STRAUSS

New York
Charles Scribner's Sons

Printed in the United States of America
Library of Congress Catalog Card Number 71–37220
SBN 684-12770-9

"What is this world?
Heaven above, earth below,
air between, and wind
joining them."

TAITTIREEYA – UPANISHAD

"Heaven and earth are out of communion
and all things are benumbed. What is above
has no relation to what is below, and
on earth confusion and disorder prevail."

1 CHING, Hexagram 12 : Heaven above, earth below

ACKNOWLEDGMENTS

To the following friends I would like to express my thanks:

First to John and Betty Eskell who urged me to try and write a book in the first place;

To David and Karin McPhail who discovered me at the LeConte School PTA and sent off my unfinished manuscript to Scribners;

To the McPhails, Jean Nandi, Lloyd Street, Lenore Friedman, Rosalind Grossman, John Paterson and my most faithful critic, my husband Herb, for their endless and constructive reading of the manuscript in all its stages. Their friendship means more to me than I can say;

To my brother, G. S. Sachdev, the Musician, and to his music;

To Sheila, who saw Death sitting in the corner;

To Dhruti Chaudhri and Ashok Kerr, for their translations of the songs in Monsoon;

To my editor Norman Kotker and his wife, Zane, whose enthusiasm has been a warming presence throughout; and

To Dr. Sharan Borwanker, my mentor—for existing in this world.

There were four friends who died, much too soon, during the writing of this book—their deaths have forced me, again and again, to confront Death. To them, Peace.

CHELLIE RAVOO
ANATOLE SCHAFER
ANSHE RAMAKRISHNA
BARBARA SCHNEIDER

Finally, I would like to acknowledge the participation of a psychiatrist I knew at a hospital where I was working. He said to me one day,

"Look outside—is it cloudy or is it sunny? Well, if it's cloudy, it can't be sunny—and if it's sunny out, it can't be cloudy. It's either one or the other. It can't be both."

It was as a direct result of that conversation that I left my work at the hospital and began to write this book.

"Now the real treasure....is never far away;
it is not to be sought in any distant region;
it lies in the innermost recess of our own
home, that is to say, our innermost being.
But there is the odd and persistent fact
that it is only after a faithful journey to a
distant region, a foreign country, a strange
land, that the meaning of the inner voice that
is to guide our quest may be revealed to us."

Heinrich Zimmer
MYTHS AND SYMBOLS IN
INDIAN ART AND CIVILIZATION

This book is for my husband and our three
children who took first that journey, and then this
journey, with me.

EARTH BELOW,
HEAVEN ABOVE

PART ONE

EARTH BELOW:

The Servants

1 *Summer*

THE SUN CLIMBED HIGHER into the cloudless sky, merging earth, sky, and air together in its dust-laden glare. Relentless, the heat-heavy rays pulsed, fanning the flameless fire which devoured the very air itself. The air was stifled, still. There seemed no way to escape it, to step beyond it. It stopped your breath, parching to dust all that it touched.

On the path before me the heat trembled, distorting the countryside into shimmering waves. Everything seemed shrouded with a fog of muted glare, and, panting, I wheeled my bicycle into the shade of a mango tree that stood alongside the path. I mopped the back of my neck with the edge of my sari and pinned my braid up higher on my head.

I seemed to be there alone under the blazing sun. There was nothing to disturb the heat and the stillness of the burning plains, a stillness that seemed to fill the entire space between the plains of the earth and the plains of the sky. Clasped together, the land and the sky pounded with the haze of silence and the lonely chirrup of brittle-bodied crickets. Wetting my lips with my tongue, I could taste the dry grit of dust between my teeth, and I wheeled my bicycle out of the shade and onto the path again.

The Lal Bahadur Shastri Institute of North India remained

open during the summer, although most of the students and staff had left the grilling plains before the worst heat of the summer. Those left—a skeleton staff, the house servants, the creatures from the fields—were now sleeping through the midday heat, curled in the close darkness of their bedrooms and mud huts and reedy lairs. Along the paths the concrete bungalows were shut tight against the withering heat of the merciless sun, and an occasional scavenger dog could be seen panting shallowly in the shade of a covered veranda.

My husband David and I had chosen to stay on the campus for this summer, probably more out of curiosity than any other motive. The summer before we had gone, with the others, into the cool Himalayan hills, but this year we decided to brave it in the plains. Our friends had looked skeptical when we announced our decision to remain, but David had claimed with bravado, "It can't be all that bad. We've been here a year already, and we ought to be able to take it."

"If you are not accustomed, it is very bad," they had all warned us, shaking their heads at each other knowingly. But all the same, we had stayed.

The Lal Bahadur Shastri Institute, or LBSI as it is called, sits in the midst of the fertile plains of the Ganges River, an oasis of culture and modern technology in a desert of teeming poverty, superstition, and crowded darkness. It was like a hub of hope— the hub of a yet nonexistent wheel—and it was the job of those at the Institute to send out spokes of education and development into the crowded plains around it in the north of India.

David had been asked to come as a visiting scientist, and he worked at the Institute teaching classes and conducting research with the graduate students and fellow staff members. I had originally planned to teach school on the campus, but had soon unpredictably found myself working as a nurse!

"An ersatz nurse who trains on the job," David would tease. But really, he was right. I was not trained to be a nurse, but when I had seen how glaring the need for medical attention was on the part of the local village people and the campus servant people, I had decided that that was what I would do. Armed at first with only a bottle of aspirins and a simple first-aid kit, I had gone into the surrounding villages, reading nursing books at night and asking questions of the doctors at the campus hospital until they finally took it upon themselves to give me some elementary training. And now, after almost a year of working amongst the servant people and the local villagers, I felt as at home with syringes and midwifery kits as I had previously felt with primers and blackboard erasers. But it was the people whose lives I had entered with whom I really felt at home.

In fact, it was to see a young servant that I was going out now in the heat of the midday sun. He was a houseboy, working for our friends, the Venkataramans from Madras, but I was told that he was now staying at the quarters of his father, who was a cook working for the Chakravortys, the Bengalis. I knew the father, Ram Dulare, fairly well, for I had seen him often when visiting with the Chakravortys, but his son Rudra I had seen only once or twice. He was a strong-looking boy, tall and well built, and it was hard for me to imagine him stricken down. And he was a stubborn fellow, too, I remembered, thinking of the stir he had caused on the campus last monsoon—a stir amongst high caste and low caste alike—by falling in love with a young girl who had wandered onto the campus in search of work, forlorn and homeless and worst of all, dark-skinned. His father had forbidden the marriage, declaring that his son could not marry out of his caste; but Rudra had defied all and had taken this young Padma —without dowry, without family, without a thing to her name— and had married her in a ceremony of his own caste.

I remember seeing Ram Dulare at the wedding, resigned but proud, watching the proceedings from the side while his jaw worked spasmodically. He had watched guardedly while Padma, delicate and frightened as a bird, moved tremblingly about the

sacred fire, draped in a red sari borrowed from her new sister-in-
law, Shanti. Her eyes had been cast down as she circumambulated the fire, the glass bangles denoting the new bride chinking
on her arms. Rudra had risen, his chest heaving with tenderness
and defiance, and had followed her seven times about that fire
while his father watched with burning eyes and Shanti kept a restraining hand on her father's shoulder. It was hard to imagine
that this same Rudra could be lying so sick that Ram Dulare had
to care for him in his own quarters, and I squinted at the sun,
pushing my bicycle forward against the stifling press of heat.

It was my own servant, Jagdish, who had told me about Rudra's illness. That morning Jagdish had stood stiffly before me,
his pointed white cap sitting square on his head and his eyes
fixed intently upon a crack in the wall above my shoulder.

"*Mem sahib,* yo veddy sick boy," he had begun.

I waited for him to continue, but he had kept his eyes on the
wall, his mouth pursing soundlessly.

"Yo veddy, veddy sick, *mem sahib,*" he finally repeated.

"Who, Jagdish?"

"Yo veddy sick," he insisted. "Ram Dulare come to me and
he say, 'my boy Rudra yo veddy sick. He no eat, no drink yo two,
three day.' Veddy, veddy sick, *mem sahib.*" He shook his head
pityingly, his eyes still off my face. Shrugging, he continued,
"He just yo servant boy, he can wait."

Now, pulling my bicycle along under the throbbing sun, I
passed the old tank, its dry bed cracked and strewn with debris.
The land on which the LBSI stood had formerly belonged to two
adjacent villages, and it still held vestiges of the old village days.
Wells and ancient Hindu shrines still peeked out from among
the tall grasses of the now-empty fields and from the concrete
structures of the modern buildings. On the periphery of the campus, life continued uninterrupted in the time-fashioned manner:
squatting women with manure-covered arms patted cakes of

fresh cow-dung into shapes for cooking fuel; men followed teams of water buffalo through the fields, shouting as the earth was raked up by wooden furrows; water was drawn up from hand-dug wells in pot-bellied brass vessels. And each year, following the change in seasons, the people continued to be attacked by small-pox, cholera, and typhoid, while they entreated their gods with prayers to spare them one more season.

I passed an old shrine to the god Vishnu which was now al-most effaced by dry reeds and creepers. Its reclining idol was en-circled by the cosmic serpent to which these villagers had been devoted, and I wondered where the people of this land had gone when their village had been taken over by the modern Institute. They had not gone anywhere, I realized, but still haunted their own land, working as grass choppers and construction laborers, milk sellers and gardeners for the campus—and household serv-ants, I mused, thinking of Ram Dulare and his sick son, Rudra. Here, on the same land, they wandered, strangers, staring out from hollow eyes and blending with the dust in their ragged saris and stained breechclouts.

Pushing with all my strength against the press of heat before me, I wheezed in strangulating breaths, feeling my energy drain out of me with each push of the pedals. I reached Chakravorty's gasping, the perspiration dripping beneath the rims of my sun-glasses and my skin prickling and clammy. The path to the serv-ants' quarters behind the bungalow was thick with powdery dust, which had blown there from the withering garden. I stopped for a moment, dizzy and panting, to lean against the bungalow and catch my breath, but the concrete burned at the touch, and rub-bing my arm I stumbled on to the servants' quarters behind the house.

The servants' quarters, two parallel barracks of three rooms each, lay beyond the bungalow and housed six servants and their families. The barracks were joined by a narrow strip of earth which lay between them—of dust or mud, depending upon the season—and together formed their own compound. Laying at an uncanny angle from the main house, the servants' quarters were so effectively separated from the house by a walled court and kitchen garden, that they were not visible from either the house or the lane. It was an incredible feat of engineering, and in fact, it was possible, by sticking to the lanes and the walled compounds, to avoid ever setting eyes upon the dwellings of the servants or upon the servants themselves, who could slip discreetly from their rooms into the kitchen doors and back again without ever being noticed.

I stood now indecisively in the dusty strip between the two rows of doors, not knowing which belonged to Ram Dulare. I coughed against the parching dryness in my throat and unscrewed my thermos bottle when one door opened a crack and the dark face of a young woman, Shanti, the daughter, peered out at me.

"*Mem sahib hai,*" she muttered to somebody in the room behind her. "The white lady is here."

She nodded gravely towards me and opened the door just wide enough to admit me, covering her head with the end of her threadbare sari before closing her palms together in front of her face in the *namaste* gesture of greeting.

She watched me, her eyes contracting with curiosity and fear, and the silver bangle in her nostril flashed like white light against the deep brown of her skin. She and I were about the same height, and both wore our hair in a long, black braid. At Rudra's wedding people had teased her about looking like me, like the white *mem sahib,* but her eyes flashed above raised cheekbones, and her burnished brown midriff was firm above her sari skirt, which was a striking contrast to my soft and rather rounded look. She moved across the room, her bare feet stepping firmly on the earth floor and her faded purple sari swishing about her ankles. The red *tika* dot on her forehead stood out like a third eye as she darted looks towards me to see my reaction to the sight of Rudra, who lay, wrapped in a sheet, upon the *charpoy*.

The *charpoy*, a cot of woven hemp, stood in the corner of the dark, bare room, and a shrouded figure upon it was tossing fitfully and moaning. The stench of diseased flesh was overwhelming, and a single lightbulb cast a greenish glow that did not quite extend to the corners of the room. Ram Dulare, the father, squatted beside the *charpoy*, his face expressionless and his wrist rhythmically fanning the flies from his son's body.

"Namaste," Ram Dulare greeted me in a hoarse voice, lifting his gnarled hands and the reed fan above his forehead in salute. He held his lips tightly together, and the fine lines about his eyes were stretched in strain. He looked helplessly down at his writhing boy and continued fanning, rumbling deep in his throat and spitting a ball of phlegm into his slack hand.

Shanti turned to me supplicatingly and said in a low voice, "Rudra. He is sick."

"How long has he been sick?" I asked in a whisper, my eyes catching on the gaudy prints of Hindu saints pasted onto the walls.

"It is almost two weeks," she answered almost inaudibly.

"Does he take water?" I asked quickly. Her eyes darted at me, crinkling with fear.

"Not for these two days." She cringed backwards. "That is why we have called you."

Sharply, I whispered back, "Never wait that long again! My God!"

I bent over to look closer at the boy on the *charpoy* who was wrapped, corpselike, in a white sheet. His body began to tremble feverishly, and a swarm of buzzing flies hovered in the air above a pus-stained patch on his bony head, which Ram Dulare swatted at with vicious strength.

"Unwrap his face," I demanded, my stomach sinking in anticipation of what I would see. Shanti glanced at me piercingly before obeying, and Ram Dulare turned his face away, his eyelids drooping with fatigue. The cloth stuck to the wound and had to be pried away, with bits of scab and pus coming away with the sheet. Immediately the black flies clustered about the open flesh, and both Shanti and her father flung their arms about the air above Rudra's head to keep the flies away from him.

Rudra's strong young face was gaunt and twisted in an agony of pain and delirium. Above his right eye, which was swollen and closed, stood a raw, purple wound extending up into the scalp above the hairline. The flesh oozed with yellow pus, and the edges were scaly and festering. I lifted his head gently, and pulling out my flashlight, examined the wound more closely. Rudra twisted in my grasp, groaning fitfully and pulling at the sheets wound about his arms. Shanti continued fanning at the flies, and her father stood shakily and placed the weight of his arms upon his writhing son, looking up at me with helpless eyes and swallowing hard in his throat.

The wound looked to me as if it had begun as a minor cut or boil. Boils were not uncommon during the hot season, but there was always a danger of infection entering even the smallest sore through the fine and polluted dust blown about by the hot, relentless winds. In fact, one of the few things that thrived during this season of dearth was septic flesh, and it was not uncommon to see minor sores develop into major sicknesses. Rudra's wound seemed not only to have gone septic, but the infection had apparently spread throughout his system, and I realized, feeling weak, how close to the brain it was.

Gingerly touching the wound with one experimental finger, I said, "Give me some water, please."

I could not take my eyes off his face. It was almost unrecognizable, and as I slid one hand under his neck, his open eye rolled in its socket, his head wobbling heavily against my arm. He struggled against the tightly wrapped sheets with uncontrolled movements, and Ram Dulare held tensely onto his tossing limbs, pressing against them with his futile weight. Shanti handed me a brass jug filled with water, and I held it to Rudra's lips. His tongue lopped out of his mouth, and he uttered low grunts, his Adam's apple working convulsively in his neck.

"No, that won't do," I muttered. "Bring me a piece of cloth."

"Padma!" Shanti called sharply to a figure in the corner. Padma rose unsteadily and came uncertainly towards the *charpoy,* her face hidden behind the edge of her sari. "Padma, bring a cloth," Shanti ordered.

I had not even noticed that Padma was in the room! The corners were in shadow, and she was so small—smaller even than I had remembered her. Her tiny frame seemed to be completely taken over by her protruding belly. She looked to be at least seven months pregnant, shrouded in a faded sari with only the ends of her toes showing. She swayed heavily forward and bowed to me delicately, her frightened eyes peering out at me from behind the cloth draped low on her forehead, and moving to where a line of rope was strung across the room, she fumbled through a small pile of cloth garments that were tossed across it. She found nothing and turned to us helplessly, but Shanti was turned away towards her brother. Padma grasped the edge of her sari and sharply tore off one piece of it, handing it to me nervously and slipping quickly back into the corner of the room, where she sank to the floor and continued to watch me out of frightened eyes.

Holding the ragged bit of cloth in my hands, I felt even more helpless, but I dipped it into the water and let it drip onto Rudra's dry lips. He responded by staring wildly and drooling dried spittle from his twitching lips. Ram Dulare held onto him more tightly, and I let the water drip sloppily onto his mouth, wetting his chin and cheeks until his tongue flew out in an uncontrollable search for the water. And from deep in his throat came a gargling moan that rose and grew into a bestial roar of agony.

Shanti held her ground and stopped fanning. Ram Dulare

lifted his face to me, still embracing his son, and tried to speak, but no words came from his voice. His mouth worked helplessly and then he gave up, burying his grizzled head in his son's sheets as the roar was followed by a convulsive shivering that took over the boy's body. Rudra's jaws clamped shut, and his shaking grew in intensity as his body was taken over by a twitching fit of delirium. I stood back helpless, transfixed by the sight of Rudra's convulsion. It ended with a hiss of pain, his chest heaving with labored breaths and his face bathed in sweat and tears.

"Is that the first time?" I asked.

"No," responded Shanti, her voice low.

"Why didn't you call me the first time?" I choked out in a dry whisper. There was no answer.

"Why?" I insisted.

Shanti and her father looked uneasily at one another, and Ram Dulare answered, "We are not allowed to go to the hospital. So now we have called you, and now you have come. But still, Rudra cannot go to the hospital. So what is the good?"

My heart sank. Of course he was right. Being a servant, he was not entitled to use the campus hospital. The rule was that neither servants nor villagers could use the facilities of the hospital. That was the reason I had begun working here in the first place.

"But . . ." I began futilely, and having no argument to offer, I stopped.

Shanti spoke in a flat voice, "We thought to bring him to the city to a doctor, but the city is so far, and in a rickshaw . . ." she trailed off. In a stronger voice she continued, "When we are sick we must care for ourselves. As we did in the village. It is God's will."

I looked from one to the other. They stood beside the *charpoy* and stared stonily at the walls. Padma was huddled in the shadows, too scared to move. Rudra lay breathing heavily, the flies still hovering in the air above him. Reaching quickly for my bag,

I turned towards the door and mumbled back at them, "I will go
and get help."

The searing glare of the sun struck me with renewed force. I
gasped against the heat, feeling smothered both by my panic and
by the blast of scorching dust that rose from the wheels of my bicycle as I pedaled frantically towards Vera Bloomfield's bungalow at the other end of the campus.

Vera was an American doctor who had come to the LBSI at
the same time as we had come. She was, like David, working as a
visiting technician, and she was assisting with the administration
of the campus hospital. This was her first summer at the Institute—she had escaped to the hills along with the rest of us last
summer—and it was with both relief and trepidation that I raced
my bicycle towards her house to ask for help.

She lived alone in one of the large bungalows set off from the
rest and reserved for very high-status staff. *"Rajpat,"* we jestingly
called that section of the campus, "Road of Kings." She was a
tireless worker and devoted zealously to "doing good for other
people." As time wore on, however, I had noticed that although
her efficiency was unshakable, her selflessness appeared to be
curling bitterly at the edges, often leaving her petulant and re-
sentful of those people she could never quite think of as human.
I hoped that today she would not be defensive, putting me off, as
she often did, by looking down at her wrist watch while I spoke
to her.

I arrived at her bungalow, my cotton sari disheveled and
streaked with dust and perspiration. I wheezed heavily as I made
my way up the path past the wilting palm trees on the front
lawn to the tightly bolted front door. At my ring, the door was
opened immediately by her servant, who must have been dozing
in the cool darkness of the hall near the door, and tottering dizzily through the open door, I entered the cool and shaded hallway.

"*Namaste,* Chhotey Lal," I greeted her servant, whose baby I had helped cure of worms only two weeks earlier. "Please bring me some water." He padded to the refrigerator on bare feet, bringing me two tall glasses of precious boiled water, the only kind of water I would dare to drink in this season.

"How is your family?" I asked pleasantly between gulps. "How is the *baba* feeling?"

"*Tik hai,*" he answered formally. "It is well."

He stood stiff and obedient, ready to carry out any order that I might give him. A proper, upper-class servant. I waited for him to offer some less formal news, but he stood upright and silent, waiting for my command. If his wife and child were ill in the back quarters, I thought to myself, he would also have answered, "*Tik hai,*" and then gone to Jagdish in the night to let him know that he needed my help. Which was, of course, what Ram Dulare had done.

Vera had taken care of his baby, but on the general subject of caring for servants she would say, "I agree that it is a pity that they are excluded from the hospital, but the policy, basically, is a sound one." And her right eye would wink nervously, and she would enunciate very clearly, using her hand for emphasis, "An institution can either handle a limited number of people well or an indefinite number of people badly. In my opinion, a job should be done well or not at all!"

And thus Vera had wiped her hands of all responsibility towards the servants. It was probably futile for me to be here asking for her help, but it was my only chance on the campus. Tomorrow I would take a rickshaw into the city and visit some of the doctors there.

With my heart beating fast, I turned to Chhotey Lal and said, "Go wake up *mem sahib* Doctor. Tell her there is an emergency."

He rushed up the stairs relieved to have an order to obey, and shortly I could hear the clear measured tones of Vera's Chicago-Hindi responding to his murmured message. Even straight out of

sleep, I thought with admiration, she can summon her meticulous Hindi! Within moments she appeared at the foot of the
stairs, immaculate in a blue shirtwaist dress, her short graying
hair combed neatly about her ears and low-heeled sandals on her
feet. She looked coolly towards me, her air of unruffled virginity
broken only by the deceptive nervous wink of her right eye,
which always made me want to smile and wink back in daring
complicity. Immediately I became self-conscious of my straggling
hair and the dark perspiration that dribbled down my sari blouse.
Rumpled and sweating, I fidgeted in my chair, tongue-tied before
her spotless sterility. Even in this weather she didn't seem to per-
spire!

Vera broke the uncomfortable silence, asking me crisply,
"How are you, my dear?" Her cool blue eyes flicked over me, and
just as I found my voice to answer, she looked down at her wrist
watch. My heart pounded in my throat, keeping the words from
coming. Why had I come here? What use would it be? I wished
I had never set eyes on this woman!

But seeing my agitation, she relaxed and came to sit down
next to me.

"What is it?" she asked kindly. With a sinking sensation I realized that it was my discomfort that made her kind. Had she
been fidgeting and nervous, then I could have been the one to be
kind! I still could not speak.

"Chhotey Lal, bring *mem sahib* some juice," she called out towards the kitchen.

Suddenly, in a rush I blurted out, "It's a matter of life and
death! You've got to come, Vera. Please come!" And then I
stopped dumb.

She raised one eyebrow and said professionally, "Yes?" She
was focusing on my chin, carefully avoiding my eyes, and I didn't
know where to begin.

"You know Chakravorty—the Chakravorty in Bengali literature? Well, it's his servant's son. Do you remember that boy

who picked up a waif and married her and everyone was so
upset? Well, yes, it's him—that boy." I stopped for a breath and
continued in a confused rush. "It must have started as a boil—
over his left eye—no right eye—and it went badly septic, and by
this time is systemic."

She raised her eyebrow again, with supercilious indulgence,
and I blurted out, "He's delirious and dehydrated and I'm sure
he's got meningitis!"

She looked at me with a cool smile, and checking her wrist
watch in an automatic gesture, announced with tight lips, "We
never make a diagnosis until a proper examination has been carried through." She got up stiffly. "If you tell me where he is, I
will go and have a look at him."

I shrank thankfully back into the cushions of the chair and
waited until she gathered her bag and gave orders to her servant,
and then followed her out into the scorching sunshine to her
waiting jeep.

Climbing into the jeep was like walking into a furnace. The
seat burned to the touch, and the wheels churned swirls of dust
from the dry gravel, which clouded the air around and settled
grittily between my lips. Vera's jeep was the only motorcar on
campus this summer—except, perhaps, for the old ambulance,
which was occasionally seen rattling through the lanes to the
hospital. Vera's driver nodded sleepily and stepped on the accel-
erator as Vera leaned forward and announced, "Chakravorty's
bungalow. Type Two section, please."

She sat back, careful not to touch me with her shoulder, and
cleared her throat. Her unringed fingers tapped sharply on the
leather bag in her lap, and she glanced down at her wrist watch
with a self-conscious smile. I looked out the window on my side,
squinting against the glare and raised dust, and itched sweatily
by the time we reached Chakravorty's house.

"Wait for us here," Vera told the driver, and nodding briefly

to me, she stepped out of the car and straightened the back of
her crease-resistant dress.

not sari

The shock of the sun hit us both with its scorching intensity,
and we both gasped involuntarily. Small rings of perspiration
began to show on the crisp dacron of Vera's dress, and pulling a
folded handkerchief from her waistband, she dabbed at her forehead.

"I say," she made an awkward joke, "we have come from the
frying pan into the fire." I laughed with effort and led the way
up the dirt path to the servants' quarters in the back.

Shanti was waiting for us. She stood behind the door peering
out into the compound, the edge of her sari across her mouth
against the dust. Her eyes flashed a shy smile when she saw us,
and she stepped aside, bowing formally to Vera as she let her
into the room. Looking at me, behind Vera's back, her face expressed the hope and fear which, at this point, she realized we
both shared. She smiled and led me in, graciously offering water
to both of us from a brass vessel. Both of us declined. *(not boiled ?)*

The small room was suffocating with its dark, pervasive
stench. Near the floor in one corner a single tap dripped disconsolately onto a clogged drain on the ground. A *chula,* or mud fireplace, and four dented brass vessels indicated the kitchen, and except for that, the *charpoy* upon which Rudra lay, the strung
clothesline, and the Hindu gods on the walls, the room was bare.
The heavy darkness seemed to hold droplets of sickness in sus-
pension, forming a slimy coating about its occupants—Ram Dulare, Shanti, Padma, and the shrouded Rudra, who lay shivering
on the *charpoy.* Vera moved close to me and cleared her throat
uneasily.

"I will just have a look at him," she began in English, opening her bag and slipping a rubber glove onto her hand.

"Take those cloths away from his head," she ordered Shanti in

Hindi, who bent down in a single motion to obey her. Ram Dulare squatted by the cot and looked up at Vera as if she were the
incarnation of a god—the answer to his prayers. Vera ignored
him and adjusted her spectacles, peering down to look at Rudra's
uncovered face. The wound was blotchy and red, and it attracted
a swarm of flies that buzzed and circled above Vera's head. Ram
Dulare took the reed fan from Shanti and knocked clumsily into
Vera, shrinking apologetically away and muttering a stream of
Hindi to Shanti.

Vera's mouth was set in a hard line of concentration as she
probed with her gloved finger about the edges of Rudra's wound.
Her breath came in unconscious whistles, when suddenly Rudra
arched, baying like a hurt animal, and set to shuddering violently
beneath the cloths. Vera stood up, dismayed, and laid a restraining hand upon the sheets; but the convulsion had taken hold,
and it rose to a frothing, tossing peak, Rudra howling against the
restraining sheets, his body flailing helplessly upon the *charpoy*.
As suddenly as it had started, the convulsion stopped, and a yellow gush of urine spread soakingly through the cloths, wetting
Vera and attracting all the flies in the room. Vera jumped back.
Her eyes wide, she mumbled, "These people . . ."

Rudra's good eye opened and fixed itself deliriously upon
Vera. It searched her face, desperate. She turned away, pronouncing medical terms. Rudra's eye burned towards her, watering and
bloodshot. His mouth drooled, and from his throat came inhuman sounds of anguish. His pain clutched out towards everyone
in the room. Vera never looked back.

"What do they expect one to do now?" she complained.
"Why do they let things go so far? This case is hopeless!" Her
voice trailed off in a note of genuine despair, and she began to
close her doctor's bag. Ram Dulare and Shanti stood hopefully in
their places, absentmindedly fanning at the flies. She turned towards them and scolded, "Why didn't you bring him to a hospi-

tal before this?" She tried to control the disgust in her voice. "Why did you wait?"

But all of us knew the reality of the situation. The campus hospital was closed to them. The city hospital was hopelessly overcrowded, understaffed, and filthy. Everybody knew that those places were where you went to die, not to get better. A poor man like Ram Dulare could do nothing else but turn to his god. Sometimes his prayers were heard, and sometimes they were not heard. Or he could go to Jagdish in the night and beg him to send his white *mem sahib* to look at his son.

Vera was thoughtful, her chin cradled in her palm and her right eye winking heedlessly. Her blue shirtwaist dress dripped with perspiration as she squinted down at the panting Rudra. Padma stared out from her corner, her lips parted as she looked disbelievingly at the long white legs of the woman who stood over her husband. The only sounds in the room were of Rudra's breathing and the whining of the flies. The drops of water from the tap hit the drain noiselessly, and the heavy air throbbed.

"Couldn't just one exception be made?" I whispered hesitantly to Vera. "I know there's at least one bed available . . ."

Vera turned to me sharply, suddenly alert. "And have fifty others on the doorstep tomorrow? No! No! You know that is impossible!"

I shrank back, disappointed. But she continued in a gentler tone, "Let me try this. I will contact Gupta at the hospital in the city and ask him to look after the boy personally. He will do that, I believe." She looked thoughtful. "Then I could come and see him too." And still thoughtful, she walked over to the tap near the floor and turned it on to wash her hands. The stream of water roused a sizzling swarm of mosquitoes that had been settled on the wet drain. In a haze of wings they rose and set like stinging soot all over her arms and face. She backed away with dismay, slapping at her arms and shaking her head wildly to loose them. Shanti and Ram Dulare jumped forward and fanned ineffectually at her, bumping into her as she tried to back away from the whining insects. I picked up her bag and herded her out of the room as quickly as I could, rustling her hair and shaking her dress to get the mosquitoes off. Back in the jeep the bites began to swell like pink blotches on her pale skin. Neither of us spoke, and she stared directly ahead of her as the jeep turned the corners of the lanes towards her house.

"I'm—I'm sorry," I began.

"Never mind," she mumbled, as if she wanted to say more. Again, neither of us spoke.

"Look, Vera," I began again, "do you think we could use your car to get him into the city?" Vera turned and looked at me with hurt and anger in her face.

"He can use the ambulance, if you insist," she retorted icily. "I would say that we are doing enough for these . . ." she trailed off, not finishing her sentence but drummed nervously against her black bag with her fingertips.

The sun at dawn rose behind a gray haze, a white disk, colorless and opaque. The air was still to become stuffy with the heat of its yellow rays, but at five o'clock in the morning the air was relatively cool and fresh. Jabbering flocks of parrots flew raucously towards the grove of mango trees, followed by crows and black myna birds in formation; and behind them came the chattering parakeets, to spend their day in the shade of the thick-leafed trees.

At the horizon a glassy band of red light began to separate the firm earth from the dimensionless sky, and then broke up slowly into layers of pink shadow that cushioned the rising sun and joined, again, the land with the skies.

I tucked nervously at the loose edges of my cotton sari and watched as David checked through my bags and thermoses to make sure I was bringing everything I would need during this open-ended day in the city.

"Will two thermoses be enough?" he asked skeptically, kneeling on the front lawn in his sloppily tucked *lungi,* a length of cloth knotted about his middle. He looked up at me with sleepy eyes, his disheveled hair and beard framing his face, "Look, you have no idea how long this day is going to last, I want you to take at least one more filled with ice cubes," he insisted, straightening his lanky body with a snap of little bones. "I'll get it," he said over his shoulder as he moved towards the door gingerly on bare feet, "and what about money, do you have any with you?"

I smiled at his retreating back, impatient to be off. David was even more nervous about this ordeal than I was, and he returned with the extra thermos and a stack of paper tissues and lemon drops.

"You might need these," he said, stuffing them into my bulging bag, and with the ice cubes rattling reassuringly in the thermos, he walked me to the end of the lane and then padded back to the house as I continued swiftly on towards Chakravorty's house.

Chakravorty was out on his lawn when I arrived, his *dhoti* draped between his legs and hitched high on his fat thighs, and his sacred thread stretched over his full belly. He grunted as he stretched his arms high over his head in the position of the yoga sun worship, and then bent slowly towards the ground with palms together, his bottom voluminous in its many folds of cloth. I waited at the edge of the lawn while he stretched flat out on the dried earth and arched his back voluptuously towards the rising sun, his face bright red and sweating.

"*Namaskar,* Chakravorty," I greeted him.

"Ah! Ah!" he puffed, purple with effort, and got up and waddled towards me, his pudgy hands outstretched. "To what an honor do I owe this visit? Hanh? You jasmine blossom." He waved his hand magnanimously towards the horizon, "You and our Lord the sun have arisen together, and both have come to me!"

His wife came out onto the lawn, still crumpled in her sleeping sari, and she shot him a look of pouting disdain, which he conspicuously ignored. He held me with his fat-cheeked smile while she plucked fresh jasmine from the flowering bush on the lawn, and he asked, "What brings you here?"

"Rudra is sick," I replied, "Ram Dulare's son. We are taking him to the hospital in the city."

Chakravorty's earlobes shook, and with dramatically downcast eyes, he murmured, "Ah, I know, I know—poor chap." He shook his head back and forth piteously.

"He's in your quarters, you know. Have you been back there to see him?" I asked.

"Oh! Ah . . ." he replied quickly, "yes, I know. No, I did wish so much to go have a look at the chap, but such work they give you around here, I tell you, one has hardly time to breathe." He mopped at his brow with the back of his hand, rolling his eyes upwards and shaking his head. "You are taking him to the hospital?"

"Yes."

"He will have a doctor look after him there?"

"Yes."

"Then that is just perfect!" He was beaming again. "Then there is nothing to worry about! It will all come out fine, isn't it?" He pumped my hands sweatily and turned to squint at the sputtering Institute ambulance that rattled around the corner and stopped in a choke of dust and gravel in front of the bungalow.

"There you are," he announced triumphantly, and immediately twisted his body into a new contortion, closing his eyes and breathing deep, rhythmic draughts of air that caused his flabby nipples to quiver on his chest.

I waved to the driver of the ambulance and then started towards the back to rouse the others. Even from that distance I could smell the reek of the ancient ambulance, and I hoped we would make it into the city before the sun got too high in the sky. Halfway along the dirt path to the back I stopped short. Directly ahead of me, kneeling before a tiny altar built from a clay flowerpot and river stones, was Shanti, deep in her prayers. She was squatting, a figure of faded purple and rich copper skin, her strong-boned face hidden in the moving shadows of her hands. She tossed grains of rice and petals of jasmine onto the flowerpot, whispering sibilantly and bowing, with her head to the ground. Her long braid shone down her back as she moved with definite grace through the ritual of the morning *puja,* sprinkling the last of the holy water onto her altar. Then, rising quickly she hurried back to the room.

I came forward slowly, but she noticed me, and turning she whispered, *"Mem sahib."*

Her eyes flashed and changed their lights several times in that moment of greeting. Then they went noncommittal and guarded. "He is ready," she said flatly.

I tried to picture her in another existence—nurtured, fed, protected. Beyond the poverty and deprivation lay the potential of great beauty, and the intelligence in her dark eyes was unmistakable. I had heard that Shanti was engaged to be married soon. The boy was from Lucknow, a city boy. Apparently, Ram Dulare had been saving a dowry for his only daughter since her birth in village days and was now negotiating the match with the father. The match was supposedly well above their station, and for this reason Ram Dulare had not permitted Shanti to work. "To work would down-caste her," he would say. The dowry was considerable, I was told, and as soon as the matter was finalized between the two fathers, Shanti would leave this place and go to live with her new husband's family.

I must have stood musing with an air of growing sentimentality, for she looked me up and down with brusque impatience and said again more sharply, "My brother is ready. He is going to the hospital, no?"

I followed her into the room where Rudra lay on the *charpoy* swaddled in fresh sheets, a sacred stone clasped in his unfeeling fingers. A bucket of food for the day stood beside the cot, and Padma stood at her husband's head, caressing his shoulder with both hands, which she pressed together in greeting when I entered the room.

"Will you come?" I asked Padma, who was breathing in little shallow gasps over the burden of her protruding belly. She looked at Shanti and answered, "No, *mem sahib*. I will stay with Ram Dulare to prepare his food."

"I will come with you," Shanti informed me unsmilingly. "Father will work at the Chakravortys, and Padma will stay with father. Let us go."

Ram Dulare came hurrying from the Chakravortys' kitchen to see us before we left. Looking at my face beseechingly, he placed both hands before his forehead and bowed long and deeply, the way one does to a deity in the temple.

Crossing the spur-line railroad at the entrance to the LBSI, we turned onto the Grand Trunk Road and joined the stream of men and animals, of bullock carts and wandering holy men, that has surged down this main thoroughfare of North India since the beginning of time. As always, the road teemed with herds of goats and water buffaloes, hoarse-voiced herdsmen with well-used sticks, wandering cows and jangling *tongas,* the two-wheeled carts pulled by emaciated ponies. The clamor of wheels and voices, the creaks and bleats and hoofbeats, seemed to slice through the odor of fresh excrement that hovered in the air from the fields and the roadsides.

The morning mist rose on either side of the road, the meager chaff of the fields giving up its night-time dew to the rising sun. Like dark dots the squatters in the fields lowered themselves and then rose again, relieved, the water vessels in their left hands empty. Amongst them the scavenger swine waited, obscene and beady-eyed, the little untouchable girl who herded them beating them together with a long stick. Women waited at the roadside wells, brass vessels balanced on their heads, their bare feet ankle-deep in fine dust. Barefooted cyclists pedaled through the crowds, sounding their jangling bells and calling hoarsely to the unwary walkers in front of them. And through it all skulked the dogs, the mangy scavengers that competed for the bits of trash that lay trampled in the thick dust.

The old ambulance wheezed jerkily through the crowds, the driver accelerating expressionlessly through all obstacles. Shanti and Rudra were in the back, in the van, where Rudra lay upon a narrow cot on the floor, and I sat up front in the cab with the driver, straddling lumps of sprung horsehair stuffing that were spilling from the old leather seat. I had to brace myself against the chipped dial panel as the ambulance lurched and swerved precariously through the crowds, finally jolting to a sudden halt behind a rallying rickshaw.

"Black idiot!" yelled the driver, holding his palm against the piercing horn. "Get going, you crooked-legged bastard, or I'll smash your machine to a hundred pieces!" A half-naked boy was bent over his broken rickshaw, the black awning on the back tipped off its hinges and the front wheel bent as though it had been hit by another vehicle.

"But he's got a broken rickshaw!" I protested, seeing the look of fear in the young boy's face.

"Heh, heh, heh," the driver snickered obsequiously. "I get you to hospital in hurry." He leaned hard into the seat, stretching his arms against the steering wheel and sounding the horn impatiently.

We passed the roadside village at the peak hour of the morning market, and the crush of people and animals just about stopped our progress. The sun was inching its way above the horizon, and already the heat of the day was upon us. I dabbed at my perspiring neck with the end of my sari and looked out the window at the crowds of people milling and haggling with the *wallas,* or merchants, at the market. The vegetable *wallas* and the grain *wallas* cried out in a cacophony of hoarse-voiced song,

> "Onions, onions onions, eight *annas* only;
> Turmeric, coriander, chili, coconut;
> Two *rupees* per kilo, eight *annas*, eight *annas* only.
> Cheap corn, cheap corn, cheap corn. . . ."

The voices faded into the noises of the crowd as we made our way past the market place and onto a clearer stretch of the road. The driver slowed down and, with an embarrassed snicker, said to me in awkward English, "Your honored pardon—heh, heh—for me to stop here in village—heh—for *bidi.*"

"Uh—I guess that's all right," I answered, thinking that this stop for his cigarettes was a good chance for me to have a look at Rudra. "Please don't be long, though." I said. "The boy is very sick."

He swung the ambulance to the side of the road, routing a couple of villagers who stood gossiping over their sacks of grain and fodder, and then flung himself out the door with hardly a backward glance, running into a roadside stall across the road where kettles steamed over fire pits and men in dusty drawers squatted on their heels.

Rag-clad boys—the ubiquitous rag-clad boys of India—began to gather about the ambulance, standing in small knots and watching every move I made. I had begun to get out, but their numbers were growing imperceptibly as they stood, speculating and giggling, their eyes never leaving my face. They stared and whispered amongst themselves, and then a boy jeered out loud. The others turned to him encouragingly, and they all laughed, watching me. Where was that driver?

"Namaste," I attempted nervously, holding my palms together out the window.

Nobody moved, but as stragglers continued to join them they began to come closer to the ambulance, surrounding it and finally touching its sides, running their hands along the boxlike van and finally, all together, trying to rock it. Rudra groaned from inside.

"What's in there?" A boy asked sharply.

"A sick man," I answered uneasily, "Going to the hospital." I glanced towards the tea shop, but the driver was not in sight.

"Let's see him," they badgered, the word 'hospital' moving through the crowd in murmurs. They came up more boldly, touching the wheels and trying handles, and hearing the back handle of the van turn rustily, I leaped out of the cab in a panic to defend Rudra at any cost. But then I heard Shanti's voice; it was Shanti who had opened the latch and was standing on the back fender shrieking into the crowd of boys, "*Jao! Jao!* Get out of here, you low-caste vultures!" Her face burned with fury. "You bastards! Your fathers had intercourse with your sisters to get you! You come from swine! *Jao! Jao!*"

The boys fled, but not very far, and they stood in a jeering mob only a few feet away from the ambulance, never taking their eyes off us. The commotion brought the driver from the tea shop, and running across the road he grabbed up a handful of gravel and began throwing it at the boys, who scattered wildly in all directions, guffawing loudly as they ran. They stopped farther off, and the driver threateningly picked up more stones, shouting curses at them as they retreated. Slapping the dust off his hands, he muttered menacingly in their direction and climbed back into the cab of the ambulance.

His jaws bulged juicily with a wad of lime paste and betel nut rolled in a *pan* leaf, and before turning the sputtering vehicle back into the stream on the Grand Trunk Road, he spat a whistling projectile of red juice out the open window; it landed with a splat on the thick mantle of dust by the side of the road.

Back on the road, we barreled heavily through the crowds, honking rickshaws and walkers out of our way, swerving around

animals and bullock carts, and giving way to no one smaller than
our truck, until a large lorry, a Public Carrier, came up the road
towards us. It was riding the hump-backed crest of the road at a
roaring speed, scattering everyone off to the sides in a dash for
their lives. With the others we gave way, careening wildly into
the shoulders and bumping dangerously into the roadside
ditches, jouncing and honking madly.

The Public Carrier sped past us, leaving in its wake a billow-
ing cloud of brown dust that choked the road with a blinding
screen. It would take at least ten minutes for that dust to settle,
and with the stream of traffic, we staggered slowly back to the
road at a blinded crawl. My skin tingled with the scorching dust,
and my throat was dry and parched. I drank from one thermos
and realized, with a throb, that the day had hardly begun. The
sun showed in a ring of white heat beyond the haze and had
hardly begun to climb above the fields. Alongside the road a
wrinkled elephant was being washed by a small boy who sat atop
his head, a tiny brush and bucket filled with water alongside
him, and I watched enviously as the boy sloshed the water behind the elephant's ears and scrubbed away at his thick skin. I
rubbed my sticky hands together and squelched the desire to take
another long drink of water.

Outside the gates of the hospital the venders called their
wares and swatted at the milling cows and goats nibbling at their
stalls, and the street sleepers sat blinking in the sun, waiting for
their turn at the street-side taps. Cows and haggard beggars competed for the edible flotsam on the streets, and a herd of goats
bleated its way disjointedly through the crowds, urinating stinking streams into the dust under their hooves. We made our way
through them and, entering the grounds of the hospital, stopped
short at the building where bodies in dust-shrouded cloths lay
curled in the sun, their dark skin covering the bony armor of
their still-beating hearts. The sick lay silently while their families

squatted beside them, watching the entrance door and waiting.
Babies suckled and cooking fires smoked in the unshaded dust.
The people and the smoking fires and the barren dust merged together, like so many hillocks of earth, and like the earth they
moved only when they were moved. Would Rudra have to wait
out here in the blazing sun with the others? My heart caught in a
sudden panic.

"Wait here," I commanded the driver. "Shanti!" I called
through the partition of the ambulance, "I am going to find that
Dr. Gupta and will be right back with help!" I could not hear
Shanti's reply.

The main hall of the hospital was like a vast railway station:
dark and musty with a high brown ceiling that dwarfed the
figures milling beneath it. The stained, yellowed walls rang with
hacking coughs and the shuffling of many feet, and they echoed
the twang of the creaking fans that hung suspended from the
high ceiling and the frenzied buzzing of the ever-present flies.
The huge room smelled of fear—a sour stench, brown and slimy.
A half-naked sweeper ran a dirty mop over the concrete floor,
halfheartedly dripping brown water from the bucket onto the
floor, leaving behind him a trail of slime like the path of a land
snail, which the bare feet of the surging mob immediately
effaced.

I stood near the entrance, having no idea where to go to find
Dr. Gupta. Slowly, I moved towards the center of the hall, towards the bronze bust of an Englishwoman for whom this hospital had been named. She sat complacently in the middle of the
hall, her placid bronze face seeming strangely otherworldly
amidst the haggard faces in the crowd milling about her. I read
her name absentmindedly, and was interrupted by a smiling
young man in a white jacket, a stethoscope hanging rakishly
about his neck.

"May I help you please?" he asked pleasantly, and I realized at once that I was as out of place in this hall as was the English lady benefactor.

"Yes, please," I answered gratefully. "I am looking for Dr. Gupta."

In very careful English, he remarked, "C. V. Gupta, P. S. L. Gupta or R. J. Gupta, please?"

More than one Gupta! My Lord, I had no idea in the world which Gupta I was looking for!

"I—I don't know," I answered lamely, and tittered.

He looked at me closely, figuring, and finally said, "It must be C. V. Gupta, isn't it? You want the Senior Medical Officer," and turning towards a large staircase at the far end of the hall, he directed me up the stairs and to the right. He nodded politely to me and strode off, leaving the crowd to close in on me and the bronze Englishwoman.

Dodging old men and naked children, mothers and suckling babies, cripples, blind beggars—all pouring up and down the stairway—I followed the right hallway until I reached a doorway which read:

C. V. Gupta—SENIOR MEDICAL OFFICER
M.B.B.S.   D.T.M.   F.R.C.S.

After hesitating a moment, I opened the door without knocking and walked in, panting out in a breathless voice, "Dr. Gupta?"

A kind-faced man in rimmed spectacles looked up from his desk, holding up his hand to the group of interns who surrounded him with pencils poised over small notebooks.

"Dr. Gupta?" I breathed out again, glancing apologetically around the office at the young men who stood watching me.

"Yes?" he replied quizzically.

Had he spoken to Vera? I wondered with a shock. There were no signs of recognition on his face. He was probably the wrong Gupta!

"Oh, you see, Dr. Bloomfield—I am from the Lal Bahadur Shastri Institute—she called you, I mean . . ." I began hopefully, but his face never lost its kind but quizzical smile.

"Didn't Dr. Bloomfield ring you up yesterday?" I asked weakly, feeling helpless.

He shook his head, but gently, and I continued.

"There is a boy with meningitis . . . Dr. Bloomfield at the Institute was to phone a Dr. Gupta here at the hospital to see about having him admitted, and now we have him here—he is downstairs—and he needs help right away—please!" I was almost in tears.

"Yes, yes," he responded, not unkindly but with a cloud of weariness on his face. "Yes, we will help him." He paused and motioned to the interns to leave and asked me, "There was no facility at the campus hospital for him?"

I tried to keep the edge of bitterness out of my voice as I answered, "He is a servant."

Dr. Gupta looked down at his fingernails and then cocked his head to the side, saying to me gently, "I will see to him myself. We will do all we can." Calling loudly into the hall in Hindi, he summoned his bearer and instructed him to follow me down to the ambulance and to bring Rudra to a bed in the waiting ward.

The veranda of the waiting ward was thronged with crouching and lying figures: emaciated bodies lying passive on stained cots, shrouded bones squatted against the walls, all waiting. Shanti and I followed the bearer, who held Rudra sloppily under the armpits while the driver had grabbed his legs, and ignored the stares and whispers that followed us along the veranda.

"Pakistani?" I heard the voices go back and forth. "One of our village girls with a white sister?" At that Shanti looked back at me with a smile of complicity, and we fell in step to confuse them still more.

Rudra was flopped onto a cot; he panted hoarsely. I took an ice cube from my thermos and gave it to Shanti, who wrapped the edge of her sari about it and held it to Rudra's lips. He foamed and sucked feverishly at the ice, tossing fitfully on the springless cot. The driver and the bearer stood away from the bed talking, their hands behind their backs and their eyes on the ground. In the center of the courtyard a crowd of women surrounded a running tap, letting the water fill their brass jugs and buckets and holding their small children under its stream. Tempted by the metallic splash of water in the brass vessels, the two men shuffled over to the tap and bent down to drink, cupping their palms and letting the running water spray into their open mouths.

Along the veranda, sunken-chested men and women weakly coughed and spat into the dust of the yard; young mothers suckled matchstick-limbed infants who stared, huge-eyed, at nothing. Amongst them, Rudra lay panting, soaking the begrimed straw mattress with deep yellow urine. Shanti and I sponged him with water from the tap and kept glancing fitfully towards the exits from which Dr. Gupta might appear.

The driver, his chin dripping with water, stood apart from us, smiling through bad teeth and rocked back and forth on his heels. I turned to him, saying, "You may go back now, if you wish."

He looked down at his dirty fingernails and twisted his fingers uneasily. Looking up, he snickered, "Heh—heh." His teeth were stained red and black with betel nut and decay. He shifted his weight, waiting.

"What is it?" I demanded.

He supplicated me with watery eyes and kept smiling stupidly.

"*Bakshish, mem sahib,*" he finally whined.

I had completely forgotten to pay him for the use of the ambulance.

"Oh, yes," I apologized, taking out five rupees from my purse.

"Here is three rupees for the ambulance and two rupees for you. And thank you."

He held out his hand, his head tilted shiftily towards me and his eyes pleading. The bills lay on his still-open palm, and as I turned away, he whimpered, "C'mon, c'mon *mem sahib—bakshish,* c'mon."

Confused, I tried to ignore him, but his whine persisted. "C'mon *bakshish,* c'mon *bakshish, mem sahib.* I'm a poor man, have many babies, *bakshish,* be nice *mem sahib.*"

The irritating whine and my helpless confusion made me act with sudden certainty, and whipping around in a single motion I grabbed the bills out of his open palm, threatening, "Go now—without the money!"

Taken by surprise, he reached helplessly for my closed fist which held his five rupees, and with tight lips I told him, "Three rupees for the ambulance, two rupees for you. You may have them if you leave this minute!" Grabbing for the bills with fear on his face, he bowed low and left the veranda at a run.

I felt dismayed by my own hardness, but Shanti was looking at me with open admiration.

"You told him, *mem sahib,*" she remarked, "He is a greedy swine."

"No," I countered, "it makes me unhappy to do that."

"But you did it well," she insisted, taking a fresh sheet out of her bag and carefully unwrapping the soiled sheet from around her brother. We both stood beside Rudra, sponging him and glancing around at the others waiting on the veranda, and with Rudra between us, we began to talk.

"Do you have babies, *mem sahib?*" Shanti asked with shy boldness, caressing her brother's shoulder with her fingers.

"Not yet," I replied with a giggle. "But some day. I have not been married very long." We smiled at each other, two women with a common interest.

"You are going to be married soon, aren't you?"

Shanti's face came to life, for she wanted very much to talk about her forthcoming marriage. "Ah, yes, *mem sahib*," she breathed. "My boy is a good boy. He is from Lucknow." She pronounced it "Nucklow."

"When is your wedding to be?" I asked her, noting the fine lines of her high cheekbones and imagining how radiant she would look in the bright red of the wedding sari.

"In the monsoon," she replied, "when my father makes the match final with his father."

"Has your boy seen you yet?" I asked quietly, and she looked down modestly, supressing a happy smile.

"No, not yet."

I told her, "He will be very happy when he sees you. He will love you very much."

She trembled under her coarse purple sari, and covering her head with an end of the faded cloth, whispered, "If I please him, *mem sahib*."

Shanti smiled shyly at me and slipped off the veranda towards the tap in the center of the courtyard. The sun was rising higher and higher in the sky, withering everything in its path and wringing from every particle its last hint of moisture. The air stank of heat and disease, and my stomach heaved with a sudden fit of vertigo. I unscrewed my thermos, leaning against the rail of Rudra's cot for support, and drank as much as I dared. There was still a whole day to go, and one thermos was already half gone. The water barely slaked my thirst, and again my throat felt thickly fuzzed with flannel. The water splashed from the running tap, ringing wetly against the metallic jugs like droplets of liquid jewels, and the sound penetrated my head and dripped like poison pearls through my consciousness. Shanti held her hand under the tap and drank long and deeply, and then returned to the bedside with a dripping rag, which she held to Rudra's sucking lips. No, I could not resist that water, no matter how polluted, I had to quench this maddening thirst. Just as I was about to leap off the veranda towards the tap in the courtyard, Dr. Gupta came striding onto the veranda, a bottle of Coca-Cola in his hand.

"You must be very thirsty, isn't it?" he asked me with twinkling eyes. "You Westerners cannot touch our water, can you." Surprised and grateful, I drank the warm bubbly soda steadily until it was gone, while he quickly scanned Rudra's face, lifting the edge of his coverings with the tip of his small finger.

"Hmn-n" was all he remarked. "Bearers, bring him to Ward B," he ordered the two men who came behind him with a canvas stretcher. And motioning to Shanti and me to follow him, he strode out of the veranda at almost a run.

Through crowded corridors and bed-cramped wards we ran behind Dr. Gupta, relieved that at last Rudra was in his hands, and squeezing through clusters of people we hurried to keep his figure in sight. At the entrance to one ward he stopped, looking over his shoulder to make sure that we were still behind him, and slapping his hand on the bony rump of a ribby cow that had wandered in off the streets, he said to me with a wink, "In your country it is not like this, no?"

I shook my head breathlessly and patted the cow, dodging around her as Dr. Gupta took off again briskly through the ward, passing limp bodies spread akimbo on the beds and family groups huddled around cooking pots. Chamber pots overflowed onto the grimy floor, and small black birds flitted through open windows to perch on bed railings, fluttering into the air again and out the windows on the opposite side of the ward. At the end of the ward Rudra was being lowered by the bearers onto an empty bed as, running and out of breath, we caught up with Dr. Gupta.

"Yes," he muttered, waiting impatiently for Rudra to be put in place before examining him. "Sister!" he called sharply to a nurse who was passing, "Assist me with this patient, please."

She nodded expressionlessly, tilting her head to the side in a gesture that looked like No to me, but in these parts meant an un-
equivocal Yes.

"Unwrap these cloths," he ordered, peering down at Rudra's
thin, shaking body as it emerged from the sheets. He took one
limp arm and felt for the pulse, pressing with practiced fingers at
the lymph glands in the neck and armpit and groin. Rudra
twisted and moaned, crying tearlessly from his fevered sleep.

"Badly dehydrated," mumbled the doctor. "Sister, I want an
I.V. with saline solution and dextrose right away." Running his
eyes over Rudra's body with Shanti and me standing anxiously
alongside him, he shook his head and unwrapped a blood-pres-
sure apparatus, reading the temperature from a thermometer the
nurse had placed between Rudra's lips.

"Hmm-n, yes—no good," he mumbled without looking up.
Curtly he asked us, "How long has this been going on?"

Shanti was all but hidden behind the veil of her sari, and I answered, "They told me he was without water for almost three
days, and the convulsions started the night before last." My heart
sank at his hard expression, and I went on, "I think it's been
about two weeks."

"Chhh-a-a!" he expostulated, shaking his head, "These people! They didn't want to bother you until it was too late, isn't
it?" he muttered bitterly and bent lower to look more closely at
the festering wound above Rudra's right eye.

The nurse came, pushing a squeaking metal stand rigged with
rubber tubing and solution bottles. She moved lethargically, her
eyes meandering restlessly about the long ward. With a bored
expression she fitted the needles into Rudra's wasted arms,
checking the rate of drip and twisting small valves on the rubber
tubing. Dr. Gupta ignored her, and swabbing carefully at the
edges of Rudra's open wound, he asked me, "Do they have any
money, these people?"

I hesitated, and then began to explain that there was a dowry saved for the daughter. But answering his own question, he swiftly rejoined, "No, of course they haven't any money."

Shanti looked at me and gave a deep, shaky sigh, and we both jumped when Dr. Gupta called out to the nurse, "Five grams sulfadiazine hooked into the I.V. right away!" and then, brushing his forehead wearily with the back of his hand, he said:

"It will take a lot of drugs to save him, you know." He paused. "And even then I cannot guarantee . . ." My face fell, and he continued more gently, "Why these poor buggers always wait until the last minute when it's too late . . ." He pursed his lips and continued more reassuringly, "It will take a great deal of drugs—more than we can dispense without cost, unfortunately— but if you can organize some kind of a collection on the campus . . ." He shook his head sadly.

"Don't worry about the money," I broke in. "We'll raise it somehow, but you've got to do everything you can to save him." My voice was shrill with strain, and he looked at me with interest, smiling quizzically.

"It means that much to you?" he asked.

"Yes," I replied automatically, looking down at Rudra's clenched face. His breath was coming in shallow gasps. Yes, it did mean that much to me, I realized all at once, even though I hardly knew this boy. Even if the rest of the world were dissolving about us, still right here and right now saving this boy was the most important thing in the world. I looked back up at Dr. Gupta and replied again, "Yes."

Dr. Gupta received a tray of sterile equipment from the nurse and continued to smile quizzically at me as he slipped on the rubber gloves.

"I am going to clean that wound," he said to me. "Perhaps you would like to leave. It will be painful for him."

"I—I think I can take it," I said with bravado. "I could help you hold him, if you wish."

"Good," he nodded, and turning to Shanti he said in somewhat gruffer Hindi, "Go now."

Shanti tilted her head obediently and taking a last, fearful glance at her brother, leaned towards me and whispered, "*Mem sahib,* I will go now to bring Ganesh?"

I had forgotten! There was another brother, a younger brother. It was at his birth that their mother had died, during the village days. Since Ganesh's birth, Ram Dulare had to raise the three children by himself.

"Of course," I whispered back. "Does Ganesh know about Rudra yet?"

"No, *mem sahib,*" she replied, her eyes down.

"Where does Ganesh stay?"

"He works for a family by the High Road. I will take a rickshaw and come back with him soon." And bowing towards the bent back of Dr. Gupta, she slipped quickly out of the ward, throwing her threadbare sari over her head with a jingle of the bangles on her arm.

Dr. Gupta held a sterile swab over Rudra's wound, covering the rest of the face with bleached cloths.

"Notice how deep this infection has gone," he said gravely, scraping aside pus and clots of yellowed flesh, and pressing his swab against the sheaf of muscle covering the bony skull. "It is going to take me a while to clean this up. Are you sure you can take it?"

Rudra whimpered beneath the cloths on his face, and I felt a prickling shock run up from my heels.

"Let me just take a drink of water," I breathed shakily, unscrewing my thermos. "I think I will be all right." He waited, his swab poised over the wound, and then announced gravely to the nurse and to me, "Ready?"

"*Aachaa,*" we both muttered, "Yes."

"Don't faint," he addressed me, a spark of fun in his eyes.

"Will it be that bad?" I asked falteringly.

"Yes," he replied simply. "But come here and hold onto his legs. And sister," he continued, indicating the needles that were taped to Rudra's forearms, "keep a watch on these. He is going to struggle." And as I steeled my weight against Rudra's knees, the doctor took the first scrape of his patient's wound.

Flinging and howling, Rudra arched against us as the first clot of septic pus was cut out of his forehead. The wound began to bleed afresh, soaking the cloths and dripping redly through them and into his screaming throat. Dr. Gupta steeled himself, wet with blood and perspiration, and gouged deeper, cutting and scraping at the infected area while Rudra flung with inhuman strength against us. I sat on his knees and looked the other way while Dr. Gupta continued to scour the wound, Rudra's screams vibrating through me for at least twenty minutes as his right eye and forehead were cleansed and smeared with disinfectant, and finally wrapped in many layers of bandages. Rudra lay limp, beaten, his breath almost knocked out of him. The nurse stood by, bored, her hands poised to lean again on the needles in his veins should he set again to tossing.

"Sorry," murmured Dr. Gupta to nobody in particular. The sweat poured down his face and neck. "Poor bugger," he remarked, shaking his head, and then continued more brightly, "And how are you doing? You held out rather well, I must say."

Suddenly my stomach heaved, and with a prickling flush of nausea, I lowered myself onto the bed and let my head drop between my thighs. I wanted to faint—to die. I felt I could never get up without spewing oceans upon oceans of bitterness. Dr. Gupta stood waiting alongside me, my thermos of ice cubes in his hand.

"You drink only boiled, isn't it?" he remarked, fingering the thermos with vague interest. He waited for my spell to pass, and when I lifted my head, said, "Keep that head down longer!" and calling to a passing intern, gave him instructions to bring me to his office.

"See that she stays there until 4:30," he ordered, paying no attention to my protestations. "Get her some tea and make sure there is tea there when she wakes up." And speaking firmly to me, he said, "I want you to sleep until evening. You are not to stir until I say that you may!" And docilely I allowed myself to be led to his office, and lying down upon his sweaty plastic couch, fell asleep immediately and slept through the worst heat of the day in a sound and dreamless sleep.

It was close to five o'clock when I finally awoke. My mouth was dry and sour, and my clammy body was stuck in a crumpled heap to the plastic couch. With an aching head I heard the water from the courtyard tap splash metallically into the brass pots, and irritable, thirsty, and sweaty, I reached for the pot of tea that sat on Dr. Gupta's desk. My sari was limp and creased around me, and the over-sweetened tea clung like a bitter film of sugar to my fuzzy lips and tongue. Standing, I shook out my sari and tried to clear my dizzy head, and somewhat straightened out, I made my way along the halls and down the concrete staircase to Ward B where Rudra lay.

The low evening sun cast long shadows across the darkening wards, and the hospital lay in a still hush of rhythmic breathing that rose and fell quietly in the suspended air. People lay curled in their beds, hoarsely panting through parted lips, and they lay in family heaps upon the cooler concrete floors, twitching in dreams and sighing as they turned over. A persistent cough rang out through the hushed wards, striking a sharp cry against the echoing walls like the sound of a *koel* bird calling across the plains to his mate. Through the open verandas came the hint of a breeze, giving us respite from the cruel power of the daytime sun and bringing the cooler night, with inexorable certainty, round again.

Walking past the sleeping figures I came again to Ward B, where Rudra lay sleeping fitfully under his white swath of bandages. Beside his bed stood Shanti and her younger brother Ganesh. Ganesh was holding a wet cloth against his brother's pulsing neck, listening intently as Shanti recounted for him all that had happened since Rudra had fallen ill. Ganesh stood with his weight balanced over one hip, his body naked except for a longish loincloth knotted about his waist, and his young face was framed by toppling black curls that glistened as he moved. He was about Padma's age—about seventeen, I guessed—and had the grace of a lithe young pony. The muscles in his chest articulated smoothly as he turned around and surveyed me with candid, but unusually perceptive eyes.

"Mem sahib," he addressed me respectfully, lifting his palms together in a *namaste.*

"You are Ganesh?" I asked needlessly. Shanti interrupted and with a small laugh introduced us, pointing proudly to him and keeping her eyes on his face. Ganesh put up his hands briefly again, and then turned back to his brother, his face darkening and relaxing elastically, changing like a landscape beneath a scudding cloud. He took a deep shaking breath as Shanti announced to me in a whisper, "Ganesh will stay with Rudra, *mem sahib.*"

I felt a flood of relief pass through me, and turning to Ganesh I asked, "And your people, will they give you leave?"

He shrugged, his eyes still on his brother, and he replied, "I will stay."

Rudra moaned weakly and twisted towards his brother, and Ganesh murmured to him gently, letting his long fingers slide supportingly under his brother's neck. Rudra reached blindly with the grasping fingers of one hand, and Ganesh put his face into those fingers, his features contracting with dry tears. Shanti gulped loudly and put her hand on Ganesh's back, and the three were linked together in wrenching silence, while I turned away, an outsider.

The sun was sinking rapidly, and Ganesh urged us to leave.

"Go take care of father," he remonstrated, "I will be here—you go now."

"Do you have food to eat?" Shanti asked solicitously.

"I will get food—you go now," he repeated quietly.

"We will come tomorrow," Shanti assured him, looking at me for confirmation. I nodded, and she reached for his hand, looking down at Rudra again for a last time before turning from the bed and shuffling, at my side, along the concrete corridors and through the main hall and out again into the street.

The noise and dust struck us heavily as we emerged, blinking, from the dark hall. The heat still rose in waves from the blistering pavements although the sun was spreading like liquid gold along the horizon, reflecting the ashes of the day's heat in sharp-rayed glints on every surface it touched.

Teeming mobs of men, rickshaws, carts, and animals moved steadily along the road in front of the hospital, thudding the thick dust into the air and filling our ears with sharp shouts and jangles that were dulled by the throbbing motion of the crowd. After the heat of the day the venders and beggars were out in profusion, all hawking and trailing us as we moved out towards the road to hail a passing rickshaw.

"Samosa alu!" called one, holding a greasy potato-filled pastry before our noses. They followed us with bolts of cloth, which they spilled in front of us, rolling each back expressionlessly as we walked on ignoring them. The beggars were more persistent. They followed, whining without stop, babies whimpering astride their hips, flies clustered about running eyes and running noses, all with bony hands stretching out and scraping against our elbows.

"Baba sick," they cried, touching their fingers to their pursed mouths, "Baba hungry—eat—eat . . ."

"That baby is rented—not hers," announced Shanti with disdain. "Professional beggars, all of them." She turned to the old crone who followed us and yelled shrilly, *"Jao! Jao!"* flicking her hand at her unrestrainedly.

"Please, Shanti, can't we find a rickshaw and get out of here?" The crowd seemed to be closing in on us as we got closer to the road, and I felt choked, suffocated. I still had about two inches of melted ice cubes in my thermos, and while Shanti looked out for an empty rickshaw, I lifted it to my mouth and drank the last of the water. From behind my upraised arm I heard a thump– thump, and turning I found myself looking into the pock-marked face of a young boy clad in a single rag about his waist, who smi- led hopefully up at me with hand outstretched. He was leaning on a long stick, his palm open towards me.

"Bakshish, mem sahib," he said urgently, his lips still smiling. He stood on one leg, the other leg a useless stump which had been cut off above the knee and which he wrapped like a hooked finger about the stick.

"Bakshish, mem sahib," he repeated, pressing his palms to- gether before his forehead.

"Shanti," I faltered, backing off from him. To hand him even one pice would mean twenty other beggars at my heels in an in- stant. "Shanti, find us a rickshaw."

Two rickshaws drew up at the same moment, each drawn by a stringy young boy in a ragged breechclout. The rickshaws were like bicycles, with a back seat for two behind the rider. The dou- ble seat was like a carriage, upholstered and covered by a large black awning, and the driver sat on the bicycle seat, straining his weight to pedal the vehicle forward. Both rickshaws arrived at the same time where we were standing and locked wheels, the two boys setting up a din of foul abuse as they competed for the fare. A crowd collected around us and began to take sides, argu- ing loudly over our heads as to which rickshaw had reached us first. I looked helplessly at Shanti, who grasped my hand and ducked down, slipping with me between the feet of the people surrounding us and out again a little farther up the road, where, with sharp-eyed dispatch, she hailed another rickshaw and pulled me with her into its low-slung carriage.

"Lal Bahadur Shastri Institute—up the Grand Trunk Road," she announced with cool aplomb to the rickshaw *walla,* and as we lurched forward she looked towards the crowd surrounding the other rickshaws and smiled to me with disdainful triumph.

Pitching forward we swayed from side to side as our boy-pedaler pushed his weight against first one and then the other pedal. Swerving around the obstacles of the crowd, we careened unsteadily towards the junction of the Grand Trunk Road and stopped at a stall by the crossroads where the boy bought two green pellets which he popped into his mouth and started to chew.

"What's he eating?" I asked Shanti.

"Hashish," she answered shortly. "It makes him easier."

The rickshaw pulled and wavered, jerking to a halt against the crush of creatures on every side. Behind our dark driver we jolted, moving inexorably forward through a bleating, shouting, honking scene which was muffled by a screen of earthy dust. It merged before my eyes like the ghostly silhouette of a shadowy dance, and I hung on to the side of the rickshaw, longing to be home.

Across the fields the sun's setting rays seeped imperceptibly into the earth. Sky and earth were banded in a red glow, clasped duskily together before the fall of night. The sun sank slowly, letting its red arc spread against the land, and just as it was about to disappear altogether we reached the by-road that led to the spur-line railroad. And then, in the space of a moment, the sun went under.

A stain of red lingered briefly on the darkening horizon, and then it, too, vanished. The earth and the heavens were one in darkness. In the space of a breath, all was changed. It was night.

David and I were awakened the next morning by the insolent

cawing of a black crow that stood preening himself on our window ledge, peering in with beady eyes and snapping his blue-black beak at us to wake us up. He tilted backwards when we shooed him away and circled the compound with a loud clatter of wings, only to settle again upon the window ledge with a raucous caw-caw.

The sun was already well above the horizon and was spilling its heat into the early morning freshness. Already the air was growing heavy—lifeless and still, with only the flying creatures, the birds and the insects, out and abroad. The others were behind doors, shut away from the smothering sun.

Jagdish was clattering about the kitchen, dropping things and gossiping with a companion who crouched unseen in the shade by the back door. They spoke in whispers, waiting for us to get up and tell them all we knew about Rudra. As soon as Jagdish heard us chase the crow, he was at our bedroom door with a trayful of morning tea things.

"Tea?" he asked hopefully, the tea cups clanking on the tray. We never took tea in our room, and I rolled over to David and giggled into his shoulder.

"Tea?" Jagdish repeated, his voice somewhat edgy. "*Sahib, mem sahib,* yo need tea!" David and I held onto each other, trying to muffle our laughter. Jagdish was getting worried. "Tea?" he tried once more.

David pulled a straight face and in as stern a voice as he could muster, called towards the closed door, "We will take coffee this morning, Jagdish."

Again I was setting out in the heat of the day towards Chakravorty's house, except that today my mission was to see Chakravorty himself rather than his servant Ram Dulare. Prompted by Dr. Gupta, who had suggested that a collection be taken for Rudra's drugs, I was going to Chakravorty's with the hope that he would volunteer to organize the project. I had sent a message to Venkataraman as well, asking him to meet me there. Venkatara-

man, who was Rudra's employer, was a mild-mannered Madrasi
who taught with David in the Natural Sciences Department, and
who treated life as if it were a complex mathematical equation.

The sun beat down mercilessly, filling the whole sky and
spreading glare like a yellow fog across the wide plains. I felt
swallowed by it, a minute figure trying futilely to escape its
ubiquitous sway. Finally reaching Chakravorty's bungalow, I
rang the bell and ducked into the dim coolness of his front hall.

Chakravorty the Bengali, as Jagdish called him, was like most
Bengalis. For him, the only real place in the world was Bengal.
He would say, "I do not say that *you* must love Bengal, I only
say that *I* love Bengal." But then he would add under his breath,
"It is only that you are wrong if you do not love Bengal."

He felt he was pining in these plains, and had even sent his
only child, a daughter, to school in Calcutta. "So that she should
grow up knowing that she is a Bengali," he and his wife would
say sadly, nodding to each other with homesick eyes. In fact,
missing Calcutta was the only emotion they shared. Other than
that, each kept to his own affairs: she to her house and the badg-
ering of her servant Ram Dulare, and he to his classes in Bengali
literature at the Institute and to his devout practice of morning
and evening yoga. She, herself, felt shamed by all his prancing
and acrobatics, but there was little she could do except to turn
away. After all, when she had reached a marriageable age she was
not quite as beautiful as she might have been, and her father had
searched for a long time before he came up with Chakravorty, a
match for his daughter who was of the right caste with a salary
in four figures . . . she could hardly complain.

Actually, they looked as if they might have come from the
same family. They both stood about five feet tall and swelled
plumply out of their bordered white cloths, their heavy-lidded
eyes drooping at precisely the same angle, and their mouths

pouting with the same fleshy expression. But the difference between them was that Chakravorty seemed to take genuine pleasure out of most of what the world offered him—even here in
these plains—whereas his wife could derive satisfaction only
from the troubles of the people around her.

Ram Dulare answered my ring and stepped aside respectfully
as I entered. His face betrayed nothing under his starched cap,
and I greeted him, asking how he felt. *"Tik hai,"* he answered
noncommittally, tilting his head to his shoulder.

"Rudra is being taken care of," I told him gently. "They will
do all they can for him."

"Tik hai, mem sahib," he repeated, not looking up.

"Would you like to go and see him today?" I asked.

He looked up quickly and answered, "Today I work here for
Chakravorty *sahib.*"

"In the evening we will go?"

"Tik hai," he nodded, stepping aside and padding behind me
towards the kitchen as I walked into the darkened sitting room.
Venkataraman was already there, and he stood and bowed to me
from the shadows of the room.

"Oh," I exclaimed, surprised, my eyes still blinded from the
glare outside, "I didn't see you at first."

"I am here," he said in a polite voice. He was thin and bespec-
tacled, his somewhat overbred demeanor betrayed by the nervous
finger-picking of his hands.

"Has David gone to the laboratory yet?" he asked politely.

"He was planning on working at home this morning and
going in this afternoon," I replied. "Have you heard recently
from your family?" I asked, continuing the exchange of polite
conversation.

"Yes," he replied seriously, "my wife writes that Madras is
very humid, but the children enjoy very much to be with their
grandparents." I began to ask when he expected them back, but

at that moment Chakravorty entered the room fresh from his bath, his bare feet making wet footprints on the stone floor and his scrubbed cheeks beaming at both of us.

"Ah, my friends, my friends," he exclaimed, calling to Ram Dulare for tea and turning his face from me to Venkataraman and then back again. He took my hands in his powdered fingers, and then went to Venkataraman—I thought, to squeeze his shoulders—but at the last minute he thought better of it and clapped his hands emphatically together instead.

"You must both love me very much to visit me in this weather," he said teasingly.

Ram Dulare opened the kitchen door a crack and listened impatiently to our conversation. "Tea, Ram Dulare!" Chakravorty called without looking back, the antennae in the back of his head telling him that Ram Dulare was eavesdropping.

"Tell me," he began with a broad smile, "what brings you here, my dear. Oh! I had almost forgotten, how is that boy doing?" He bent his head solicitously, and as I tried to frame the words to begin the difficult speech, he pointed to Venkataraman and claimed with sudden recognition, "That boy works for you, isn't it?"

It had begun to come clear to him, and nodding his head up and down, he leaned back in his chair, his hands composed in his lap and his eyes shrewdly guarded.

"Rudra is very, very sick," I told him slowly, and turning to Venkataraman, added, "he may not live. He is at the hospital in the city and is in the care of C. V. Gupta himself." I looked from one to the other and impressively added, "The Senior Medical Officer." They both nodded, raising their eyebrows politely.

"He is going to need great amounts of very costly drugs." Both men looked furtively at one another. "The money will have to be raised on the campus," I hinted, pausing for a reaction. There was none. "We will all chip in whatever we can, of course," and I nodded, and they nodded, and then they looked at each other and nodded. "But it is going to take even more than that." I had said all that I was willing to say, and I stopped. They sipped their tea. I waited. They each took another sip of tea. Then they both spoke at once, and each deferred to the other. They were very polite; neither would continue.

Finally Vankataraman ventured, "Of course you can count on me to do my level best." And he glanced up questioningly at Chakravorty.

Chakravorty rose and rubbing his hands together heartily said, "Need not to worry about anything!" and looked at his wrist watch with exaggerated surprise. He showed Venkataraman to the door, and after he had left, turned to me and said confidentially, "These Madrasis, they eat from their palms like monkeys!"

When I stepped out into the sunshine Venkataraman was mounting his bicycle, a wide-brimmed straw hat perched on his narrow head, and tilting his head back and forth told me in a voice of strictest confidence, "These Bengalis, they speak a s'sy language with a mouthful of s's!"

For the next three weeks the Grand Trunk Road led us towards the hub of the sinking Rudra, drawing us forward, following some blind need, and then tugging us back again to the campus and sleep. At first only David and I came with Ram Dulare and the two women, Shanti and Padma. We came every evening, and it became an inevitable part of our day to take the long ride up the Grand Trunk Road to the hospital in the city, where Rudra lay panting under the watchful gaze of his brother Ganesh. But after a few days Vera Bloomfield joined us, relieving us of the long rickshaw journey by bringing us in her jeep. And then Venkataraman came, and finally, on the fifth day, Chakravorty asked Vera if he could come along too. It was as if Rudra dragged us all towards him, just as the hub of a wheel draws the spokes into itself.

We would come in the cool of the dawn, just as the sun was reddening the morning sky with its early light, and we would come in the evening, the sun setting in a blood-red display over our right shoulders at the edge of the plains. The Grand Trunk Road carried us towards Rudra and then away from Rudra, tugging and dragging us in both directions like the ebb and flow of the tides at the edge of the sea.

There were days when we could hope; Rudra's eyes would open and he would know we were there. He would reach with a spindly hand for the swollen belly of Padma and flicker a smile; he would try to speak, beseeching Ganesh to interpret his exhausted croaking sounds for us. At these times he was there—present behind his eyes. At least he was one of us. His piercing eyes would search us, and we would open and allow ourselves to be searched, for he was a living man amongst the living. And we would sigh with relief; he would live.

But then on the next day we would come bearing fruits and grains for him, and he would be sunk deep away from us, his eyes shut and his limbs limp. And Ganesh, standing beside him through each tide of consciousness would look up at us with the warning lights of fear in his eyes, and without speaking we would place the fruits and grains by his feet under the bed.

The drugs did their work, dripping, moment by moment, their precious fluids into the blue veins of the young Rudra. They gave him strength to do battle with the disease that tried to devour him. Some days they triumphed, tipping the scales towards life; but some days they were powerless, and Rudra lay in his bed, still and unconscious. But every drop was a drop of hope, and the drugs drained, drip by drip, without stop, into Rudra's veins.

At the same time the packet of cloth hidden beneath the floor in Ram Dulare's room was drained, drop by drop, of its precious dowry money. Ram Dulare insisted upon paying for his son's drugs. "My son, my money," he would say tersely.

We would secretly deposit our contributions at the hospital
dispensary, but Ram Dulare proudly refused to accept any out-
right charity. The small extra sums that Chakravorty would slip
into his pay, those Ram Dulare would accept quietly; but when
Chakravorty offered, in front of all the others, to give Ram Dulare as much as he needed, Ram Dulare looked the other way
and refused. Chakravorty knew his man.

The heat swelled. In storms of scorching dust the winds blew,
parching the land still more. The water in the wells dropped precariously low, and buckets with endless ropes were needed to
draw up what brackish liquid there was. An untouchable boy was
murdered at a high-caste well in a nearby village for drawing
water; and the air thickened still more.

Desiccated beasts gasped over the dry land in search of fodder,
their tongues rasping dry over their teeth; men and women
shuffled through the dust, wheezing and shrunken, their mouths
covered with grimy bits of cloth against the blowing dust. The
children slept, bellies panting and limbs thrown aside, whimpering through cracked lips for their mothers' withered paps.
Past the silent villages we would come. Every morning and every
evening we would creep, in the jeep or in swaying rickshaws,
past the dry and silent villages.

On this evening the sun was sinking sluggishly through the
choking husks of dust at the horizon. The air was lifeless and
still, no longer giving us the breath of evening respite we had
come to expect after the scorching day. Humidity had crept into
the air, weighing it down with oily cobwebs that clung, inescapa-
ble, to every particle of dust. Clouds had begun to gather beyond
the brown haze, and they hung there motionless, imponderable.

There seemed to be little hope for Rudra, but still, there was
always the chance of a miracle. Like the relentless sun at the edge
of the plains he seemed to be sinking, and treading towards him,
our hearts numb with dread, we came despite ourselves. Nobody

knew why Chakravorty and Venkataraman continued to come, nobody had requested that they come; but somehow, in the end, we all went together. For better or worse, we seemed to be in this together.

Ram Dulare had left on his bicycle while the sun was still fairly high in the sky, shedding his starched white uniform and pedaling off in string-tied drawers and tattered undershirt. He had insisted upon leaving early, offering no explanation, his reasons hidden behind his age-filmed eyes. The rest of us leaned, sweaty arm against sweaty arm in the jeep, mopping ourselves with rumpled handkerchiefs and squinting against the stinging dust: David and I in the front with Vera, and Shanti and Padma squeezed in the back between Chakravorty and Venkataraman.

The evening traffic on the road moved listlessly. Men and animals alike stood panting in the meager shade of the roadside trees, and the women stood patiently by the wells, their empty vessels balanced motionlessly upon their heads. As we approached the crossroads we ground to a halt, the road blocked by a crowd of people all concentrated on one spot. The driver leaned out of the window and sounded his horn to disperse them, but they remained pressed against each other, focusing upon something in the circle of open space.

"Get moving there!" he yelled, sounding the horn with irritating persistency. A few men lifted their heads at the noise of the horn, but none moved from where he stood. Shanti was the first to see the cause.

"Look," she exclaimed, pointing to the tops of the trees by the side of the road. There, in the high branches, loomed several hunched vultures, perched like macabre fruit with ominous intent. Stained beaks against black bodies, they came flying in, stirring the reeking air with their huge wings, darkening the sky before settling heavily upon the branches of the surrounding trees. Mean and hungry, they waited. Beneath them on the road lay a

wounded bullock beside a splintered cart, staring patiently at the
milling crowd, its severed haunch pouring blood into the dust of
the road. It made no sound, but by its side its grizzled owner
wept. He lay his head against the beast's body and he cried, curs-
ing the cruel heavens and brandishing his fists towards the driver
of the Public Carrier, which was vanishing into the distance of
the road ahead. The crowd stood about him, curious but unmoved. It could have happened to any one of them; but it hadn't.
They watched as he wept, fingering the jagged edges of his broken wheel and sobbing deep and disjointedly in his throat. They
moved aside when he rose, raying outward and leaving the man
with his broken wheel and dying animal in the center.

The vultures waited, shifting restively in the trees until the
poor beast gasped its last breath, and then in one motion spread
their enormous wings and descended, drooling, to the warm
meat. The sky was effaced by their seething bodies; down they
came, down and down. One atop the other they covered the car-
cass of the bullock and stripped it, in minutes, with their raven-
ous beaks, until it was nothing but a dusty skeleton.

We sat in the jeep, stunned. Nobody said a word. Then the
driver started up again, honking the horn and inching his way
slowly through the parting mass of bystanders, coming on steadily as each obstacle removed itself slowly from our path. We
routed an old man who, clad only in turban and ragged breechclout, was trudging blindly down the center of the road, his chin
buried in the white hairs of his sunken chest. We came honking
up to his heels before he started wildly, jumping with fear and
surprise to the side of the road, and we jolted on.

The rim of the sun was disappearing rapidly beneath the horizon, turning the uneasy light of dusk to night. Along the roadside candles and oil lamps were sputtering into greasy flames, the
sparks taking hold slowly before burning with a steady light. At
the horizon a red haze melted the edge between the earth and the

sky as the wheel of the sun rolled out of our sight, and steeped in our own thoughts we sat, withdrawn from the others and full of foreboding.

Turning slowly through the gates of the hospital we were met on all sides by the ever-present beggars, who pressed against the jeep, whining and cajoling, their hands extended, and their eyes pleading. The driver honked furiously, but they clung to the car, calling to us. There was no place to put one's eyes without seeing them; there was no possible way to avoid either their presence or the arrogant noise of the horn. Vera looked straight ahead of her, her lips fixed in a tight grimace and her right eyelid drooping spasmodically. Chakravorty and Venkataraman neatly ignored the scene outside the window and mopped at their perspiring brows, while Shanti and Padma, lulled by the rhythmic jouncing of the motorcar, had their eyes shut in a half sleep. David turned to me, his kinky hair disheveled and lines of sorrow narrowing his deep hazel eyes, and then he leaned out the window and entreating the beggars, shouted, "*Jao bacche, jao!* Go away children, go!" But they stayed with us until we had stopped at the entrance to the hospital and had gotten out of the jeep, pushing past them and into the main hall. At the door they left us, letting their whines droop into a cadence of automatic whimpers, and with dread holding us together we walked towards Ward B where Rudra lay.

Ganesh was feeding Rudra as we approached, supporting his head with one arm and placing bits of wet food into his open mouth with the tips of his fingers. Rudra opened his mouth unseeingly, like a baby, allowing his brother to put the food between his lips, his eyes fixed trustingly upon Ganesh's face. Ganesh moved in an unblinking trance, pinching up bits of potato and thrusting them gently between Rudra's wet lips, and he looked up briefly when we entered, nodding gravely at us.

Vera went to the other side of the bed and took Rudra's wrist between her fingers, counting the pulse on her wrist watch. Ganesh stopped and looked at her as she clucked her tongue professionally and took a deep sigh. He held his food-caked fingers poised in mid-air.

Rudra lay sprawled on the bed, his cover thrown aside, revealing the dull gray pallor of his legs under the sheen of sweat. His shallow belly rose and fell rapidly as he sucked in his breath and let it out again. The bandage above his right eye had been removed, exposing a bruised, purple wound on his forehead like an off-center third eye.

We stood profoundly still as Vera knelt by Rudra's side, listening to his heartbeats through her stethoscope and peering into his eyes with her small light. Her expression was grave with concentration. Then she looked sharply up at us, commanding, "Get Gupta, please!" Padma, who stood beside David, swayed off balance and began to topple in a swoon. David put a restraining arm about her shoulders, and she tossed her head, reviving enough to move towards her husband and sink to the side of his bed beside Vera, who was listening closely to his heartbeats through the stethoscope. Becoming aware of Padma beside her, she awkwardly put her hand on Padma's little head and patted her like a puppy. We all waited around the bed in silence while Ganesh ran off to find Dr. Gupta, the order having caught each of us in the place, deep down, where our nerves come together in a knot. Rudra lay between us gasping, and he drew us towards him like the vortex of a whirlpool, holding each of us inextricably in his silent sway.

Shanti stared, standing over her father, who squatted beside the bed near Rudra's head, her knuckles tense and white as she grasped her father's shoulders. Her eyes were fixed on Rudra, while Ram Dulare stared into nothing. Chakravorty stood on the other side of the bed near David, rocking on his heels and darting his eyes about the ward for distraction, trying to catch the glance of Venkataraman, who stood quietly by the foot of the bed, his eyes fixed on a spot on the white sheets. Both men tried to focus uncomfortably on anything but the twisted face of the boy in front of them, but neither succeeded, and were drawn back again to Rudra. Vera and Padma knelt side by side, the one woman tall and white-skinned, the other tiny, overburdened, and dark, both waiting anxiously for Ganesh to return with Dr. Gupta, both too afraid to look up.

Suddenly Rudra moaned, tossing weakly, his frothing lips soundlessly pronouncing, "Ganesh . . ." Everybody turned around to look towards the doorway at the end of the ward. Ganesh had still not returned. Vera again took his pulse, concentrating hard on her wrist watch; Ram Dulare's eyes contracted into slits, and the furrows in his cheeks deepened; Chakravorty coughed loudly into his handkerchief, and Venkataraman picked nervously at his fingernails. I moved closer to David and took his hand—it was cold and both our hands were shaking. We did not dare look at each other.

Rudra moaned again and Vera jumped up, pressing his eyelid open and peering down with her light at his eyeball, which swam yellow in its socket. Shanti covered her mouth with her hand and held down the noises that rose into her throat. Padma swayed on her knees and caught herself by burying her head in her husband's sheets. Vera fumbled quickly through her bag and drew out a syringe, which she squirted first into the air and then into Rudra's wasted shoulder.

Dr. Gupta hurried in with Ganesh following close behind and he asked her, "What is that?" Vera showed him the ampule and he nodded. She retracted the needle, and we all hung, suspended in the sucking whirlpool and held together by the shadowy web of fear.

Suddenly Rudra's eyes flung open. They were lucid and piercing; they saw us! Sharp edges of light illuminating them strangely, they traveled slowly from each one of us to the other. They found Padma first and rested long on her, as if remembering, thinking; they rose to Vera, who stood above Padma, the

empty syringe dangling uselessly from her fingers, and they traveled patiently towards Venkataraman, who stood at the foot of
the bed. Chakravorty followed the eyes to Venkataraman and
then twitched uneasily as Rudra's eyes reached him, finally
leaving him to rest briefly on David, and then on me.

Shanti and Ganesh stood together above Ram Dulare, and Rudra's eyes reached the three of them, resting long with each one,
receding into a far-off memory and lighting into focus as he
watched them. Rudra's eyes encompassed Ganesh's face and
stayed there; the two brothers stared deep into each others' eyes
for a motionless time. Not one of us breathed. And then Rudra
shifted his gaze, staring straight ahead but no longer looking out.
His open eyes looked inward, but then, for a desperate moment
they returned, piercing out at us, shrieking, trapped, like an un-
comprehending animal.

"WHY?"

And with one final widening of earthly terror, they shut.

Ram Dulare's grizzled head dropped forward, against the bed.
Dr. Gupta bent swiftly down to feel Rudra's pulse.

"He is still alive," he muttered hoarsely.

Again Rudra's eyes wrenched open, searching each of us rapidly in turn, while we stood, frozen with helplessness, around
him. In each of our eyes he found the dazed spectre of his own
terror.

"WHY?" was his last message to us.

"WHY?" was all that each of us could send with him before
his eyes closed for the last time and left us behind.

Death stopped his breath. Rudra had stepped beyond Death.
Dr. Gupta lifted the sheet and held it in his hand before placing
it over Rudra's breathless face. Shanti stood stiff, held as if by an
invisible wire which strained against her natural weight.

"Not yet!" she choked out at Dr. Gupta, grasping his arm and
staring, transfixed, at her dead brother's face. Dr. Gupta waited

and motioned to Vera, who stood unblinking by the bed, to take
care of Padma. Padma had slumped to the ground in a faint, unnoticed by everyone, and with a start Vera came out of her trance
and knelt to examine Padma with professional concentration.

Dr. Gupta lifted the sheet gently over Rudra's face. Shanti
shrieked, and grabbing the edge of the sheet with her hand, collapsed onto her dead brother. Sobbing hysterically she gathered
him into her arms, talking to him and keening through her tears,
kneading his body with frantic fingers and burying her head in
his neck. Carefully, Dr. Gupta pulled her away from the body
and put her into the arms of her father, who still squatted on the
floor, his eyes staring unseeingly ahead and his face betraying no
emotion.

David and Venkataraman and Chakravorty and I stood apart
together, in painful shock and helpless silence. I felt numb and
breathless. Ganesh stared unbelievingly at the place on the
sheets from where Rudra's eyes had last looked up at him; he
had not moved from the spot, and his eyes were fixed on the
spot. Suddenly, something made him jerk his head to look, startled, into the corner beside the bed. His face went gray and his
eyes widened in panic, the muscles tensing in his shoulders. I followed his eyes to where he stared. In the corner I saw nothing
but a yellowed wall, a pile of dirty linen, a spider web. But Ganesh continued to keep his eyes frozen to the spot, as if something were there. I moved over to him, but he never noticed my
presence. He narrowed his eyes and kept his gaze directed towards one spot in the corner of the room.

Dejected, and in silence, we filed out of the ward; Chakravorty, Vera, Venkataraman, David, and I. Silently we left the
hospital and drove back along the Grand Trunk Road towards
the campus. The others stayed behind to prepare Rudra for the
funeral in the morning. In the morning we would all return and
go with them to the burning *ghats* by the Ganges.

Outside, the night dogs bayed and the night coughers hacked and spat. The humidity was sweltering, but I shuddered with cold as the shock of real fear descended deep into the molten place within me where I was alone. For a moment my body tingled with the exact, pure knowledge of my own vulnerability, but then it was gone. I held onto David, seeking company, but I had touched the place where I was unutterably alone, and although David tightened his grasp around me, I felt no relief.

The jeep pulled up in front of our bungalow, and insensibly we got off. Chakravorty and Venkataraman had been dropped at their houses, and now Vera was alone in the car. As the jeep drove off down the road, she appeared smaller and smaller, seated alone in the back seat behind her driver. I could imagine her reaching home and could see how her servant would stumble up from his sleep on the kitchen floor and let her in, knocking sleepily into walls and straightening his pointed cap as he came. The house would be dark save for one burner on the stove where Vera's supper would be simmering, and Vera would climb the stairs, switching on lights as she went and stepping out of her shoes when she reached her bedroom. The table would be set for one, and Vera would unfold her napkin, waiting for her servant to dish out the steaming rice onto her plate, and nodding briefly to him, she would pick up her fork and eat.

David and I went numbly into the house and directly to bed, after having some curds and tea for dinner. We tried to talk, but kept drifting off, preoccupied, still holding onto the separate dreads within us. We slept restlessly, turning often to relieve the strain in our limbs and not succeeding in drifting to sleep until the far-off glimmers of the dawn began to stalk, like creeping cats, across the night sky. We slept briefly, but soundly, finally awakening when the glimmers persisted against the press of dark, rousing us out of our drugged, but dreamless sleep.

I tried to resist the dreadful dragging sensation I felt, wishing only to retreat further into sleep, to remain senseless. I closed my eyes tight against the stalking light, but David shook me awake, his eyes impatient.

"Get up," he demanded. "Vera will be here in fifteen minutes."

Reluctantly I let him pull me out of bed, and I draped myself in a light cotton sari and plaited my hair high on my head away from my neck, my fingers working automatically.

"*Sahib,* yo awake?" knocked Jagdish at our bedroom door, his voice small and scared.

"Yes, we'll be out in a minute," called David through the door. "Jagdish, will you have some tea ready and fill all the thermoses in the house with water."

"Veddy good," mumbled Jagdish, shuffling off towards the kitchen. I came to the kitchen, fixing the last pleats of my sari as I came, and Jagdish looked up with mournful eyes and pointed to a cluster of strung flowers that sat upon the counter.

"Garlands," he announced. I touched the flowers, shuddering for a moment at their cool, fleshy petals, and he continued, "I yo make. For the boy-—you, *sahib,* give them to the boy." His lips betrayed a quiver of pleasure at my surprise, and he nodded his head affirmatively, touching the garlands protectively and pointing at me.

We filed out the front screen door—Jagdish, David, and I— and waited for Vera. The stars were beginning to fade, and the darkness was slowly and reluctantly breaking up in the silent sky, giving way to the reddish glow of the unrisen sun. The jeep clattered up, crunching hard against the gravel of the road and braking with a screech in front of us. Vera opened the door on her side to let us in, and I saw that her face was haggard and splotchy. She grasped my hand as I got in and pressed it hard.

"You haven't slept!" I exclaimed in a low voice. "Are you all right?" She stared ahead of her, her jaws seemingly clenched behind tight lips. Her throat moved as if she wanted to speak, but she restrained it, and released her hand from mine; but it shook, and I took her hand again, keeping my eyes intently on her face.

"I had the most frightful nightmare!" she finally blurted out. I waited for her to continue, but her eyes roamed from one side of the lane to the other. I glanced in front to David, but he was lost in his own thoughts beside the driver.

"What?" I urged her in a whisper.

"Oh, you know . . ." she began impatiently, brushing me away with her hand. But then she gave way and continued. "It was certainly like a nightmare," she began, and then protested, "I rarely dream, you know." Her eyes sank away from me, as if returning to the place of her dream, and she shuddered.

"It was a cellar," she whispered, "no, a cell—like the shape of a coffin and only large enough for one or two persons." She paused and swallowed, reluctant to go on. I waited. "You see, I wasn't even too scared, except that it was so damp and quite dark," she continued. "But apparently, I escaped. I don't know why I even tried, for it was hopeless, but I knew there was a door somewhere, and somehow I tried to get to that door." She looked up at me for recognition, and then down again quickly.

"Oh, this is silly," she said.

"What happened?" I asked.

"Well, I'm not sure," she spoke almost inaudibly. "But somehow I made it out through all sorts of tunnels and alleys to a place where there were keys, and I got hold of some keys and somehow one of them opened this huge door," she looked from her dream to me, and then back again, "and I opened the door . . . and well, on the outside all there was was . . . well, a tomato! It was as if the whole world outside was a big red tomato and the seeds were spilling out," she stopped and kept her eyes down. "But then I was back inside that dark cellar, in this little cell again." She sighed shakily.

I waited and she continued, cracking her fingers, "It seems that I kept escaping and getting to the door and then finding I

was right back in the cell again, and then finally I got to the door
and the keys weren't there!" She looked up with a stricken face
and immediately composed herself, remarking coolly, "It was a
strange dream. Probably brought on by the heat and all this tension." She looked down at her lap, and mumbled hoarsely, "I
rarely dream."

I was struck dumb with her dream and deeply touched that
she had told it to me.

"That was a very vivid dream," I choked out, not knowing
what else to say. We were both silent. In fact, her dream had
evoked in me an image of a repeated dream I used to have as a
child, a dream that haunted me for years.

It was of a forest, dark and filled with ancient trees, where I
stumbled alone. There was no end to the forest—no beginning
and no end, only impenetrable darkness through which I wandered. As Vera recounted her dream, I was filled with the mysterious darkness of my ancient forest, and as we sat beside each
other, bumping through the lanes towards Venkataraman's
house, I knew that the deep cellar from which Vera ran, alone,
was identical to the dark forest in which I wandered. The difference was that outside of the deep fastness of those ancient
trees I walked the world with David; but beyond Vera's dark cellar she had to face the free fall of her existence all alone.

When we reached Venkataraman's house, he was waiting outside his bungalow, his shoes in his hand and his white trousers
neatly pressed. He greeted each of us with a grave bow before
climbing carefully into the front seat with David, and stretching
his neck uneasily, he stared out the windshield until we reached
Chakravorty's house.

Chakravorty popped his head out of the door as we drove up,
tucking in his *dhoti* and making complicated signs to us with his
fingers. He disappeared inside, and then his wife plopped two

shoes, a lunch bucket, and an umbrella on the doorstep. Chakravorty appeared again, slipped into his sandals, stood undecided a moment, and disappeared again into the house. We waited. David yawned and Vera held down a deep sigh. Again he emerged, stuffing something into the waist of his *dhoti* and gesturing at his wife, who scolded him in a loud whisper from behind the doorjamb. Bending over, he picked up his umbrella and tucked it under his arm, then picked up his lunch bucket, and looking about him to make sure he had everything, he came towards the car beaming with satisfaction. Seeing us, his face dropped appropriately into mourning, and with great ceremony he bowed and climbed heavily into the back seat of the jeep, dragging his bucket and his umbrella along with him as he did so.

We took off again, through the campus and out across the spur-line railroad and onto the Grand Trunk Road. Chakravorty looked about him with lively interest, and centering himself upon the two padded bones of his buttocks, he pressed his right thumb against his right nostril and breathed deeply through his left, losing himself rapidly in his morning yoga.

The Grand Trunk Road was peopled with wraithlike wisps; silent silhouettes slipping like shadows through the fields towards the wells. Piles of fresh excrement sat, like small gifts, at the sides of the road. Shadows emerged and retreated, floating in slow motion through the mist as water from the wells splashed uncannily through the haze, a music transparent in the dust. Jagdish broke the silence.

"Kaise hai?" he asked the driver. "How goes it?"

"Tik hai," was the short reply.

Again all was still save for the rumbling of the jeep. We passed the crossroads where the bullock had been struck down and swerved around the dust-covered skeleton, which still lay amidst the remnants of the broken cart, a man from the village sitting guard over the pieces. We left him sitting disconsolately amongst the dry splinters and continued on until we reached the place where the road widens as it enters the city.

The relentless sun was spreading upwards, dissolving the shadows and bringing the sharp bones of the real world into cruel relief. It dragged me closer and closer to something I was afraid to face, and I found myself hovering, in the desolate forest within me, several paces behind where my body stood.

My heart was pounding with dread when the jeep stopped in the hospital compound. Chakravorty pulled himself out and mopped uncomfortably at the creases in his neck with the edge of his *dhoti*. Jagdish followed him and then reached in to help Vera and me out of the jeep, until we all stood uncertainly on the gravel of the road, dabbing at our necks and faces and uneasily avoiding each others' eyes.

"Well . . ." ventured Venkataraman after a while.

"Where would we find them?" David asked Jagdish, who, being a servant, would probably know. Chakravorty opened his mouth to make a joke, but changed his mind before it took shape and whistled a tune instead.

"Tik hai?" I asked Vera, taking her arm as we all turned towards the hospital entrance.

"Tik hai," she responded gratefully, both eyes winking awkwardly.

Jagdish led us to the back of the building, across the courtyard and verandas, towards where the kitchen shack and the quarters of the hospital peons stood. Mud-walled sheds covered with thatch and corrugated iron surrounded the back courtyard, and tubs of runny food, around which half-naked men in ragged breechclouts moved, stood exposed to the rising sun. Ram Dulare was squatted by the doorway of the kitchen hut, talking softly to another man who stirred continually a huge pot of lentils. A stubble of white covered his dark face, and his eyes were fixed to the ground as he spoke. The other man nudged him, pointing to us as we arrived in the courtyard. Ram Dulare jumped to his feet, his expression changing to respect and submission, the back of his hand rising smartly to his forehead in salute.

"No, Ram Dulare!" I cried, confused. I glanced helplessly at Vera and ran to Ram Dulare, taking both his hands in mine, but he sank to the ground, his mouth curling, and holding onto my ankles he placed his forehead to my feet. David rushed forward, seeing my plight, and tried to raise Ram Dulare by the shoulders, but at David's touch he collapsed completely, his fists clenched over my toes and his back wrenching with dry sobs. Awkwardly I fell onto the ground beside him, and cradling his grizzled head in my lap, I let him weep wetly against me.

Shanti came from behind the shed and stood there, followed by Padma; they stood apart from the others, disheveled and dry-eyed. The women in the family of death, they were, since the night before, polluted and unclean. Both Chakravorty and Venkataraman shrank backwards instinctively as the two women appeared, but their uneasy glances towards each other relaxed when Shanti and Padma made no move to approach. Shanti stood with her legs planted on the ground, her red-rimmed eyes flashing desperately around the courtyard; Padma tottered, her ungainly body leaned against the shed for support and her eyes glazed and emotionless behind her threadbare veil. Ram Dulare's sobs were fading, and except for the sounds of his sucked-in wheeze and the scrape-scrape of the wooden spoon against the pot of sooty lentils, there was no sound coming from our little group. The men shifted their weight uncomfortably and squinted towards the rising sun, checking their wrist watches and avoiding each others' gaze. The women—Shanti, Padma, Vera, and I—stood apart, even from each other, each dry-eyed and strange. Frozen with fear, it was as if our instincts had retreated far out of reach, and we stood looking down at the ground not knowing what to do.

Ram Dulare got up and wiped his nose along his forearm as he shuffled off across the courtyard to bring Ganesh. Jagdish rose hesitantly and, casting a last look towards the other men, followed Ram Dulare behind the sheds to where Ganesh was waiting with the shrouded body of Rudra. The moments seemed to stop their course; the earth upon which we stood was empty. There was no place to hide, not a blade of covering to which one could cling. The earth was stripped bare, and upon its bare bones our hearts were exposed, left to beat hollowly without any bit of protection. Stripped we were—stripped to face the sight that none of us could face, and there was no place to hide.

Chakravorty began a careless remark; but his voice stuck, and he did not bother to clear it. Vera looked at her wrist watch, and when I weakly asked her the time, she had to look at it again. Shanti watched us almost cruelly, and Padma looked this way and that, seeming hardly to even breathe. The moments were suspended, and through them, when nobody seemed to expect it, Ganesh and Ram Dulare came around the shed with a bier of woven rushes upon their shoulders, upon which lay the tightly wound body of Rudra. Shanti watched us closely, and Venkataraman held his ground solemnly, picking mercilessly at his fingers. David stared, his hands clasped behind his back and his knuckles white. I could look up only in stages.

Rudra lay upon the reed stretcher, a white, encased figure shrouded in turmeric-stained cloths. His body was tied to the bier with orange and purple ropes, which crossed his cloth-bound chest and knotted finally around his narrow neck. The globe of his skull stood out starkly under its shroud at the end of his flat body, and the sharp outlines of his profile were visible beneath the tight winding-cloth that covered his unseeing eyes. Jagdish held the back ends of the bier and motioned to David with a nod of his head. Shocked into motion, David handed me one of the flower garlands from around his shoulder, and together we moved, on buckling knees, towards the bier with our last offering to Rudra. We lay the flowers on his chest, and they began to slip off, and with a look of involuntary horror at each other we secured them with the tassels of the colored rope that held Rudra onto his bier. Jagdish watched the procedure with satisfaction, but Ram Dulare and Ganesh bore their burden in front with unseeing eyes and patient backs.

Suddenly, from nowhere appeared three stringy-muscled men, their hair dusty and their skin very dark. They were all but naked, and they circled the body, one grasping the fourth pole of the bier onto his shoulders and the other two jangling tambourines alongside the bier. They conferred briefly with Ram Dulare and Ganesh, and glancing with faint curiosity at the rest of us who stood about, they started up a loud chant, beating upon the tambourines and stirring the stillness with their hoarse voices. At a signal they began to move out of the hospital courtyard, jangling the tambourines and singing loudly; Ganesh and Ram Dulare readjusted the poles on their shoulders, and the procession moved towards the road in front of the hospital, Jagdish, Ganesh, and Ram Dulare singing under their breaths along with the hired bearers and never looking back once they began to make their way towards the burning *ghats* of the Ganges.

"Ram nam sate hai! Ram nam sate hai!" the hoarse cries grew louder as Venkataraman, Chakravorty, and David fell into step behind the procession and added their voices to the chant.

"The Lord is truth! The Lord is truth!" The air was filled with their anguished cacophony as the body of Rudra swayed between the men who shouldered him towards the burning grounds by the river.

"Ram nam sate hai! Ram nam sate hai!" The procession moved out onto the road and through the morning traffic of the city, towards the Ganges and the final place of Rudra's earthly existence.

The women followed the procession up to the hospital gates and then stood silently watching until the men had become swallowed by the crowds. David looked back once and signaled, the two flasks of water swinging from his shoulders, his brown beard strangely out of place amongst the oiled black heads of the crowd. Shanti and Padma stood apart from Vera and me, until we all turned from the gate and finally faced each other. Shanti was restless and impatient and looked only confused when I brushed the strands of her wild hair off her tear-stained face. I took her hand, but it lay limp in mine, dry and feverish. Then her grip tightened and clung, and letting the tears flow easily from her throat she leaned her head against my shoulder and wept.

The tears in my chest welled and then stopped. I felt suffocated, trapped in my own skin. My throat was clogged with tears, but I could not cry. I had a fleeting image of a woman who sat upon a curbstone in a great city, her hair flung wildly over her head as she sat, weeping. She wept through the day and through the night, flooding the curbstone and the street and, finally, the whole world. And still she wept.

But my throat was parched closed. I could not cry.

Back in the jeep we turned into the main thoroughfare on our way towards the burning *ghats* by the river. The air was thick with an unbreathable haze of dust which the morning crowds had raised with their trampling feet. The sun rose quickly now, baking the earth again with its flameless fire. Herds of goats pressed against the jeep, stumbling over ribby cows in their path; naked children defecated off curbstones, and their excrement was immediately trampled into the dust by hooves and feet and wooden wheels. The crowd surged and dissolved on all sides of us, like a perpetual tide within which each particle counts for nothing.

We turned off the main road and into the Muslim quarter, onto a narrow cobbled street lined with stalls hanging with butchered quarters of goats.

Black-veiled women haggled with the merchants, peering with curiosity at the jeep from behind lace openings at the level of their eyes. A child darted out onto the road, and its mother scolded after it, grabbing the child by the arm and looking up at us with fear-sparked eyes from behind her lace-cut window. In a moment, she lifted the child and moved quickly out of our way to the side of the road, standing there with the child on her hip and watching us as we passed.

But before my eyes, still, was the sight of her leaning over to snatch her child, her startled eyes peering up at us from behind her black veil. That image seemed to exist in relief against the walls of my mind. It was as if, in that moment of fear, that mother reaching for her child was a microcosm, a pinpoint of fear, a central image from which the greater sorrow emanated. It was as if the single essence of that moment was like the hub of a wheel from which all things flowed. I caught my breath, suddenly realizing that each of us at every isolated moment in our lives also constituted that hublike center, that microcosm of everything else that there was. The image of the woman persisted, and I had the sensation of descending, dizzily, into an unvisited region of myself—a place of roots and questions, a place of dreams and terrors. I shook my head to dispel it, afraid. Shanti's hand came close to mine, and we clasped hands, both grateful to the other.

Sparked somehow by a sorrow I could barely handle, I seemed to have opened somewhere and was being led into a realm within myself which I did not know. I was moving towards the place where the root-stem of myself seemed to stand, where the textures and strings of my soul's colors seemed to come together in a single rod. Beneath that stem, in the fertile soil where the root follicles gathered their delicate nourishment, was the place from which the flower of my consciousness could blossom. It was from that place, from that root-filled dark soil, that I had seen the black-veiled woman lean over to rescue her child.

I looked about me in the jeep. Vera and Padma and Shanti and the driver. And myself. We seemed fixed, each of us at this moment, in this place, on this journey. We were together, but like the faceted sides of a crystal, though we touched, we were alone.

But then the crystal that we five formed seemed to pulse outward in every direction, creating rainbows of associations: other cars, other journeys, other people. And each association led to other memories—that car which journeyed to that place, and other recollections of those same people in other places still. And those other places led to still other people, other feelings, and other periods of my life. And the images flowed outward, sparking other memories and kindling wider and wider ripples of perception until I felt I was speeding on a wide-leafed bark through the deep green channels of my imagination, rushing through dreams and feelings of unfathomed times, dovetailing old feelings and new perceptions. Deeper I went into the wilderness of the many-channeled stream, speeding past dreams and fears, scooping up flashes of sensation from the fertile mud of the channel bank, hanging on to my leaf-boat with exhilaration and terror.

Clutching with sudden terror I dug the heels of my mind against the stream and stared desperately out the window of the jeep for something real upon which to fasten my attention.

What had terrified me so? Slowly I began to realize that the quality of my fear was exactly the quality I had read in Rudra's sharp-lighted eyes before he had closed them for the last time last night. That question, the demon of that fear, was what stood before me in the dark abyss of my imagination. I shuddered against it, trying to banish it from my mind, and I clung hard to Shanti's arm. Understanding something, she comforted me.

My body was still straining against the forward motion of the jeep, but the jeep continued steadily on, passing markets and vegetable carts, children and dozing holy men, whitewashed temples and naked washermen, tailors and walking women.

Reeling our way forward towards the river we came finally to the bridge across which lay the burning grounds. From all direc-

tions came chanting processions, each following a swaying bier
on the backs of four men, dark bandy legs glistening with sweat
and voices hoarse with singing. Ahead of us lumbered a fuming
bus with a corpse strapped to its back amongst the bundles and
valises. On all sides people pressed, their little ones clutched
tightly to them and their belongings tied in rags upon their
heads. Bicycles were lifted into the air above the heads of the
crowd and carried across the bridge, while the mass of people
moved in both directions at once and met in a shoving, pushing
impasse in the middle. Hoarse shouting, crying children, and the
chanting of the funeral processions filled the air. We seemed to
be stuck, with no chance to move either forward or backwards,
and the driver held his hand on the horn and with persistence
pushed into the crowd ahead, grazing through a space they but
barely opened for us, lumbering forward in the wake of the
fumes of the bus.

"Oh, I say!" exclaimed Vera suddenly, pointing out the window and then turning quickly to Shanti and Padma in embarrassment. Shanti and Padma emotionlessly followed her pointing
finger to a cyclist on the bridge who carried, upon his back
fender, a covered body strapped to a woven bier, the bier flapping
precariously as the rider wound his way through the crowds towards the opposite bank of the river. Vera turned to me sheep-
ishly, her cheeks blushing in apology to Padma and Shanti, but
they had hardly noticed, and they continued to stare dully at the
crowds, their young faces passive and blank.

The river, or rather the bed of the river, lay beneath us under
the bridge. The river itself in this season was little more than a
channel of brown water running sluggishly along one edge of
the wide expanse of white sands, its width continually shrinking.
The river sand was a vast plantation of ripening melons, and the
bleached sands glinted under the rising sun, the white acres pitted with melon plants and small, temporary encampments of
melon farmers. In the distance, near the muddy stream, curls of

smoke rose from the tiny funeral pyres, one after the other along the bank, the mourners about them looking like miniature figures from this distance.

As we crawled closer and closer to the site, we met more and more singing processions that arrived, panting and hoarse, and lined up their corpses amongst the others in the sun, waiting patiently for their turn at one of the smoldering beds of hot ash. We searched through the shouting crowds for a sight of our men, but it was not until we had actually reached the bluff overlooking the burning *ghats* that we finally saw them pulling themselves up the hill from the village beneath the bridge, bearing the burden of Rudra upon their backs.

Even from a distance it was apparent that Ram Dulare was about to drop with exhaustion, his chest heaving against his bones, the hairs standing out stark white against his dark skin. Ganesh was glancing anxiously at his father, holding out a hand to support him, which Ram Dulare impatiently brushed aside. The bier tossed and dipped unsteadily upon the shoulders of the four men as they mounted the hill, and their voices had disintegrated into wheezing barks croaked from dry throats. Seeing us waiting, they forced a last burst of energy and carried the bier to where the other corpses were lined in the sun, and they laid it down.

David and Venkataraman straggled up the hill behind them, dragging themselves and crumpled with sweat. I grabbed a thermos and ran towards them, unscrewing it and offering it first to Venkataraman, who waved it away and wearily pointed to the Ganges River, where he could drink of the holy water. He stumbled down the bank while David drank long and deeply from the thermos, his face red above his whiskers, and his lips dry and parched.

Ram Dulare and Ganesh waded into the muddy waters right before the *ghat,* while Jagdish and Venkataraman went farther upstream to perform their ablutions. Cupping their hands against

the sluggish current, they sprayed water ahead of them with their
fingers and chanted a prayer to the holy river, wading farther in
until the water was up to their waists. They both bent over and
drank out of their hands; swilling the muddy water through their
teeth and dunking and bowing, drinking and spitting, they performed the bathing ritual. Ram Dulare scooped up the water in
his hands and released it back into the stream, gathering and releasing it, his eyes closed and his lips moving continuously. Ganesh scraped a handful of river mud and dabbed a sign of mud
upon his father's forehead, and then one upon his own, and dripping with water and flecks of soot, the two men emerged from
the water with their palms folded in front of them. Venkataraman and Jagdish came out at the same time and went over to the
body of Rudra, where, with a coordinated grunt, the four hoisted
Rudra onto their shoulders and carried his bier, staggering under
the weight, down to the edge of the river for his last bath.

Lowering the bier carefully, they dipped it into the water and
held it under the surface of the water close to the bank. Amidst
the scum of ash and flowers Rudra was bathed with the holy waters of the Ganges River. Ram Dulare and Ganesh muttered
prayers and incantations, splashing water from the river onto Rudra's body until the winding cloths clung to the outlines of his
breathless body and the dark color of his flesh showed through.

Upon the bluff the women watched, remaining out of sight
from the men's ablutions. Shanti stood, tense and observant, at
the edge of the bluff, and she gasped sharply when the strong
young profile of her dead brother was visible beneath the cloth.
Padma could not watch and shrank away from the sight, allowing herself to be soothed awkwardly by Vera, who stroked
her arm. Shanti's face was set in a hard, stony stare, and she uttered a short cry when Rudra was lined up again with the others;
but suppressing the cry with tight lips, she stood her ground.

The sun climbed higher and higher into the sky, steadily approaching the zenith and shortening the shadows of the melon

plants on the bleached sands. Fever hot, it radiated its desiccating heat onto the precious remaining channel of the river, sucking mercilessly at the gently lapping scum of ash and petals that washed against its sandy banks. The spirals of pyre smoke rose upward towards the sun, dissolving lazily into the atmospheric haze and releasing the reek of burning flesh into the air. Dogs skulked about, sniffing ravenously around the funeral fires and plunging into the river for ashen remains; and they growled hideously through their teeth as they competitively lapped through the scum-filled water.

From behind us came the familiar sound of imaginative abuse, and as we turned around we heard the voice threatening, "Here, you fool, I said stop here!"

Chakravorty was shouting in Hindi at the small boy who pedaled his rickshaw. "I tell you and you don't hear!" Plumped heavily in the back, he raised his umbrella towards the shoulder blades of his young driver.

"Here was there, and I told you there!" The boy cringed under the threat of the umbrella, but jumped out agilely to balance his rickshaw when Chakravorty climbed out, tipping it precariously to one side and dragging his lunch bucket and umbrella with him as he got down. Flushed and sweating, he continued to lecture the steaming boy while he fumbled through his purse for the fare, talking continuously and pulling with one hand at the fold of his *dhoti* caught between his buttocks. Slapping a generous sum into the calloused hand of his young driver, he admonished, "Here! Next time be more obedient," and turning away he did not witness the boy's obsequious *salaam* before he leapt back onto the bicycle seat and wheeled his rickshaw away from the burning grounds as quickly as he could go.

Ganesh stood before the wood sellers, his pouch of money in his hand and his face thoughtful as he compared the prices of split wood and straw. The wood sellers sat complacently amidst the stacked logs and brass hand scales, weighing out the wood with bored faces.

"Ten kilo—wood, straw, and dung—thirty-five rupees only," a wood seller announced, his head turned idly away. Ganesh stood undecided; at least ten kilos were needed, but thirty-five rupees was so much money!

Chakravorty waddled up from the river, water-logged and plastered with mud from the river bed, and standing suspiciously behind Ganesh, he panted loudly and looked at the wood seller with a practiced eye.

"Nine kilos of wood, the straw and dung extra—thirty-two rupees," the wood seller announced, bored, shifting the wood on the scales. He fingered his toenail, challenging Chakravorty with an expression of utter finality, and Chakravorty took him up.

Sputtering loud enough for even us to hear on top of the bluff, he yelled, "Thirty-two rupees for that measley pile of worm-eaten trash? Do you think we are lunatics? Oh, we know your kind, we know your kind," and pulling Ganesh away by the arm, he remarked in a loud whisper, "It's probably hollow!"

"Thirty rupees," countered the wood seller, still working on his toenail.

"Not only are you a cheat," began Chakravorty, blowing himself into a genuine, red-faced rage, "but you're a stinking liar as well—in your mother's belly you were already a cheat and a liar!" Ganesh shrank back shyly as Chakravorty fumed on. The insults thrown back and forth attracted an appreciative audience of frustrated, heat-stricken mourners, who gathered around Chakravorty and the implacable wood seller as their feud continued.

Chakravorty clenched his pudgy fingers towards the wood seller's throat and threatened, "Here's what I think of your crooked little business here, taking advantage of poor people in distress."

The crowd standing about clenched their fingers vicariously,

grinding their red-stained teeth menacingly at the wood seller
and retreating respectfully when Chakravorty wound up for a
new foray. The wood seller did not appear to feel the least bit
threatened.

"I will give you ten kilos of wood and three kilos of straw and
dung for thirty rupees only. Not a pice lower will I go, not a
stick of straw more will I give," and he turned away, his part of
the bargaining closed.

The crowd shook their heads and turned towards Chakravorty
to see what he would do. Playing his part, he blustered angrily,
stamping from side to side and coughing loudly into his hand.
And after a dramatic pause, he motioned to Ganesh, who was
standing quietly off to the side, and he announced magnanimously, "You may take it at that price. But he is still a con-
founded liar." And stepping back with a paternal smile, he folded
his hands across his belly and watched as Ganesh stepped forward and shyly counted out thirty rupees from the cloth pouch
he held in his hands.

Padma swooned suddenly, her voice trailing into a faint gurgle
as she slumped forward. Looking around first for Vera, I grabbed
for Padma's waist and helped her to the ground.

"Shanti!" I called. "Bring my thermos from the car!"

Vera was nowhere in sight, and the driver shrugged helplessly
when I asked where she had gone. Padma moaned softly, twisting her head this way and that as I held the water to her lips and
patted her forehead with the dampened end of my sari.

"Please find *mem sahib* doctor!" I called in exasperation to the
driver, who was standing above me, peering over my shoulder to
gawk at Padma. "Please go find her." And saluting smartly, he
turned on his heel and disappeared across the bluff.

Padma's features were composed and gentle as she lay on the
ground before me, unconscious. I brushed the straggling hairs
behind her ears, for the first time since her wedding seeing her as
a young, delicate girl whose face was not distorted with fear. Her

features were finely chiseled and her burnished skin shone transparent, and I could see the pulse points throbbing gently on her
brow. She was not more than seventeen years old, but the telltale
lines of erosion, the inevitable wearing down by pain and poverty, had taken toll of her gentle freshness: the small furrows in
her forehead, the dry skin about her lips, which were slightly
parted over even, white teeth. I turned again to look for Vera,
and Padma lifted herself suddenly on one elbow, shaking her
head in bewilderment and sinking back to cry softly to herself
when she remembered where she was.

Vera came towards us, running on her long legs, clearing the
stones and excrement piles easily as she ran, her camera tossed
furtively behind her shoulder.

"What has happened?" she cried, kneeling immediately by
Padma and feeling expertly at her swollen womb. Padma lay still,
her eyes wide open with fright as Vera examined her. With a
short glance towards me Padma swung her face into her own
shoulder, like a swan, and burying her eyes shut, she wept. I
knelt beside Vera, and together we gathered the girl into our
laps, cradling her like a child and rocking her gently as she
sobbed. Standing above us, Shanti sighed impatiently, her nostrils flaring with confused emotion, and placing a hesitant hand
on Padma's shaking shoulder, she squeezed hard.

The men below us on the bank stood silently near a still-
smoking pyre whose previous corpse had been committed to the
sacred river, and while the other family completed its last rites,
they brought Rudra's body forward on its reed bier. Ganesh
raked clumsily through the coals with a long stick, stirring the
embers of the fire to life. Glancing up at Ram Dulare for approval, he placed two cakes of dung upon the coals, from which
the smoke rose immediately. As the dry dung caught into spits of
flame, Ganesh piled one log across the other on top of the dung,
alternating the logs with meticulous attention and stuffing bun-

dles of straw between them. His face was composed and dry-
eyed, but his chest heaved uncontrollably as the fire took root;
with a sudden spark it blazed upwards, creating a roar that could
be heard even where we stood on the bluff. Wordlessly, Ganesh
exchanged a glance with his father, and they lifted the dripping
body of Rudra off the ground, their knees bending under the
weight and the muscles in their arms twitching as they carried
him to the wild-roaring flames of the funeral pyre and laid him
upon it. His eyes stinging from the fire, Ganesh carefully placed
the final log upon his brother's hips and tossed the rest of the
straw over the body, holding his blackened arm against his
streaming face.

The wet cloth clung to Rudra's profile, the fire hissing and
steaming as it caught tearingly onto it. Picking up a clay pot
from the ground, Ganesh circumambulated the pyre, dabbing
ghee, clarified butter, onto the forehead, shoulders, and hips of his
dead brother, and darting out of the way of the licking flames as
he did so. At each point of the body the *ghee* helped the flames
upwards, sizzling with a sudden sputter as the fire caught. Ram
Dulare stood at the foot of the pyre, chanting deep in his throat
and tossing handfuls of rice grains onto the body of his son, the
furrows in his cheeks deepening and the sweat pouring in
streams down his grizzled body. Clouds of black smoke rose into
the air as father and son walked three times about the funeral
pyre, touching with a straw torch the four points of Rudra's
body, and chanting in quaking voices, *"Ram nam sate hai—Ram
nam sate hai—Ram nam sate hai. . . ."*

The fire shot up bright and roaring, and in a conflagration of
smoke and flames it began to consume the body of Rudra which
lay above it.

Shanti was breathing shallowly as she watched the rites of
preparation; but when the flesh of her brother was revealed
for a split second beneath the tearing fire, she lunged forward
and collapsed onto the ground, shrieking, "Aiyeeeeeeeeeeeeeee,

aiyeeeeeeeeeeee!" her primeval wail of grief striking through the air like a knife. Fighting off Vera who came to assist her, she shouted curses and growled low noises from her tightly clenched jaws. She clawed at the ground, screaming and scratching, her wild hair flying and her face distorted with anguish. Rising to her knees with her sari unraveling around her, she sprang like a wild animal at Padma, who cringed and retreated, her face tight with terror.

"Come here," she grunted incoherently, "come here." Her eyes were insane with grief as she made her way towards her sister-in-law on her knees. "Widow—the glass bangles—take off the glass bangles." And seizing Padma's arm with brutal strength, she tore off the colored glass bangles that are the symbolic jewelry of the married woman. Padma had not yet thought to remove them.

The bangles chinked against the hard mud, their round circles splintering into broken pieces. The young Padma, the child within her, was a widow. The two women, both panting hard with grief and fright, faced each other upon their knees on the bluff and looked hard into each other's eyes. Both were ready to do battle; both were wild with grief. Lunging towards each other, they clutched in a tearing, violent embrace and fell to the ground together in an agony of keening, upon the broken fragments of the colored bangles, and locked in each other's arms, they wept.

Vera stood rooted, the primeval wail of woman's agony ringing in her ears. She stared straight ahead of her towards the brilliant sun. The pyre flames were burning steadily, the stench of Rudra's wasted body reaching the bluff, the heat from the flames distorting the air into shimmering waves of smoky haze. The men all stood behind the fire, lined up, Ram Dulare closest to the river. The sun was behind them, blinding me, and I could make out the figures in silhouette through the trembling haze, Ram Dulare and Ganesh; Venkataraman next to Jagdish; Chakravorty; then David. They seemed almost to be linked together on a line beside the burning pyre, their bodies rocking up and down, waving darkly up and down.

My heart contracted hard. A dark knot of terror choked me, and screaming hysterically I flung myself down the bluff to where David stood at the end of the line in the dance of death.

"No, no!" I shrieked. "Not David! Not David!" I seized his arm, sobbing wildly. And then I, too, was on the line.

Linked together, motionlessly, at the edge of the river, we danced. Dancing in a line, we each danced alone.

The sun climbed higher into the sky, sending its heat-heavy rays outwards in all directions, blotting out earth and sky in its all-embracing glare.

We committed the black ashes that had been Rudra to the slowly flowing Ganges, waiting for the waters to carry them away and picking up a remnant of bone and tossing it farther into the stream to sink. Ganesh and Ram Dulare turned away from the river, and following them with bowed heads and aching throats, we left the burning place. We trod up the bluff to where the jeep stood, and fixed by the merciless stare of the devouring sun, we turned away from the burning grounds and towards home.

On the day following the cremation Padma was moved from the quarters behind Venkataraman's house, where she and Rudra had lived, to Ram Dulare's quarters behind Chakravorty's, two lanes over. Ganesh helped her move their meager household goods—a *charpoy,* a few brass vessels, a handful of cloth. Carrying the hemp *charpoy* on his head through the choking heat, Ganesh leaned it upright against his father's quarters and took leave of them, taking the dust of Ram Dulare's feet in obeisance and returning to his employers in the city after almost four weeks' absence.

Ram Dulare went back to work in Chakravorty's house, dressing every morning in his starched white uniform and pointed cap and returning to the little room in back only for meals and a midday sleep. Shanti performed her morning *pujas* before her flower-pot altar each dawn, clandestinely plucking petals from Mrs. Chakravorty's garden to offer to her stone gods, and swept the tiny earth floor of their room each morning and each evening. Padma crept quietly about, ungainly with her burden, a widow with no place to go, at the mercy of a family that no longer wanted her.

They each went about their business in silence, speaking only when they had to and mourning Rudra in abject solitude. They seemed not to want to share their grief—not to even show their grief. But if you happened to come upon Ram Dulare unexpectedly, or Shanti when her work was done, you might find them seated motionlessly on a sagging *charpoy,* neck slack and back slumped, the face staring motionlessly into the dust.

Only a few days after Rudra's funeral Ganesh returned, with long ashen face, from his employers in the city, and fearfully he approached his father, walking slowly towards the questioning glitter in Ram Dulare's eyes. Falling in a rush and burying his head in his father's feet, he blurted out quakingly, "Father, forgive me. I am fired."

Ram Dulare's eyes went hard, but he did not move his head. A questioning grunt came from his throat. Ganesh gulped through hard tears, unable to speak a word. His father grunted louder.

"They told me I stayed away too long," Ganesh choked out in a painful whisper, "they did not believe me." His voice was barely audible.

Ram Dulare did not move and Ganesh continued dully.

"They found figures of clay that I made during my free time, and they sent me away and said I could not come back." He looked up at his father wincingly, but his father never blinked. Suddenly Ganesh stood up, and reaching for the cloth pouch at his waist, handed it over to his father. It contained the money he had received as severance pay. He held his ground as his father reached for the pouch. Ram Dulare grimaced with rage, and raising a gnarled hand he slapped his son full on the cheek and then turned away to his quarters. Ganesh's blood rose into his stinging cheek, but he stood firm and waited until his father had disappeared inside the room before he turned towards the fields and fled into their protecting grasses.

Ganesh also moved into Ram Dulare's quarters. Now there were four people living in that room: Ram Dulare and Shanti, Padma and Ganesh—and with a fifth person about to come. Each stayed away from the others as much as he could. Padma wandered the campus, again a lost waif, except now she was a widow and with a full, uprisen womb to carry; Ram Dulare stayed at the Chakravortys' and came home only to sleep; Shanti moved about her tasks in silence; Ganesh escaped into the fields, striding fitfully amongst the reeds under the blazing sun.

We would come upon him often in the early mornings when David and I walked out through the grove of mango trees and across the old grazing meadow. The sun would still be hidden beneath the haze clouds at the horizon, and the air would still be breathable, and Ganesh would be alone, fingering the dry reeds or twitching his nose in the air like a prairie creature, as if sensing the subtle changes in the atmosphere as the dying season was giving way, day by day, to the new season about to come.

He smiled one morning as we approached him, rubbing a brittle stalk between his fingers and looking with observant eyes at the swelling clouds that had begun to form at the horizon. The pungent tang of the hollow husk prickled my nostrils, and I could hear the silent screeching of the dry reeds as they scraped against each other, moved by the morning wind. We walked on, following his eyes towards the growing clouds and becoming more and more aware of the snapping tangle of dead weeds beneath our feet and following the fluttering bodies of insects that alighted and broke the brittle stalks with their weight.

Our morning walks had become the highlight of the long, hot days. Invariably, we would come across Ganesh, seated beside a dry-cracked mud hole out in the fields or striding restlessly along some animal trail or nestled high up in the branches of a thick-leafed tree. He seemed to be watching for something—watching and listening and sensing for something that would come with the slightest breeze. We never spoke, although he always acknowledged us with a friendly smile. We began to look where he looked and to search amongst the web of weeds against the brown earth for the tiny creatures that moved there. We would follow them and notice the minute perfection of their busy bodies as they scurried over the crumbling straw. We caught the contrast of the yellow weeds against the blue sky and smelled the dry tang of the air, which each day carried a slightly larger edge of moisture in it. Each minute breeze that blew across the plains from the changing shapes of clouds sitting far in the distance touched our burning skin, and although each breeze was so slight, it made us glad. We lifted our heads towards the forming cloud heads and figured, feeling their promise in the seeping moisture of the clinging air, and we watched the vaulting sky overhead and the creeping creatures on the dying reeds, and we were glad.

In Ram Dulare's room, however, matters grew worse. Shanti's marriage had been called off by the father of the groom. Ram Dulare had gone to Lucknow with trepidation to finalize the arrangements, with less than half of the dowry money in his bag. He had brought Shanti with him to show to the father, hoping her beauty would make up for the missing portion of the dowry settlement, but the father was not interested. He had nothing against Shanti, but he would not pledge his son to a girl who came with so little goods. And so, on the spot, the whole thing had been called off.

Ram Dulare and Shanti came back from Lucknow even more taciturn than when they had left. They spoke neither to each other nor to anyone else, and again went about their business in stony silence, their faces never betraying the welter of emotions they must have been feeling. Padma kept out of their way. Although neither of them openly accused her, still she was a widow and thus the source of their bad luck. They had no choice but to keep her since she was with child and had no place else to go, but they made no attempt to hide their resentment. Ram Dulare blamed himself for having allowed that marriage between Rudra and Padma to take place from the start, convinced that all their bad luck stemmed from that bedeviled romance. He never spoke about it, but it was apparent that he was somewhat afraid of Padma, as if she were a witch who held a power of destruction over all their lives—one from which they could not escape.

But Ram Dulare would not be broken. I would find him stirring the rice in the Chakravorty's kitchen, his back proud and his filmy eyes hard, and when I would ask after the four of them, he would reply, "God is good to us. He told me not to take Chakravorty's money and we didn't. What might have happened to us if we had taken Chakravorty's money?" And he looked around at me with dimming eyes, his shoulders shaking slightly.

"I hope God will take care of you even better in the future," was all I could summon, restraining myself from grasping his hand.

The days followed in plodding succession, one upon the other, the air growing thicker, the nights hanging heavy with dense humidity. Dust-laden drops of darkness clung even after the sun was long gone beneath the horizon, and the meager breezes were choked before they reached us. The humidity closed in, suffocating everything that lived, bit by bit.

We all searched the sky for the gathering clouds, but they were still too ephemeral to bear the black heads of rain and thunder, still too blocked by the suspended dust that hovered at the horizon. The plains were like an enclosed space with no exit—a space that was filled, like a swelling rubber balloon, with hot, moist air.

The four people in the servants' quarters behind Chakravorty's house also seemed trapped. Each evening Ram Dulare would return from the house and Ganesh would return from the fields, occasionally with a small bunch of vegetables or a half-woven basket of dry reeds. They were all hungry; the heat gnawed at them and their thirsts were unquenchable. Ram Dulare's salary was not enough to support them all. Ram Dulare dug again into the pouch of Shanti's dowry money, his eyes watering as he did so. Shanti turned away and said nothing.

Their eyes began to stare hollowly, and their dry skin grew gray with oily dust. They held back the rage scaling in their breasts, and they moved rigidly about each other, trapped in each other's presence. They had no place to flee to; they had to keep out of the sun. Their breaths seemed empty and their minds, in exhaustion, grew shallow. They seemed each to be treading a narrow path along a razor edge of sanity. Like Rudra, they were as if moving towards a precipitous edge over which there lay nothing. Bottomless fear pounded against the weakened pulse of their lives, carrying them from one moment to the next, and the time seemed endless. They were reaching that edge over which, in the breath of a moment, they could fall. But they did not fall; they clung on—and it never occurred to them to wonder why.

In the far sky the cloud heads grew darker and darker. They formed and grew heavy with thunder. The child in Padma's belly stirred more and more, sapping her juices for its own wetness.

The wind raised the dust and darkened the air, tugging with its wind-breath at the fallow dust. The trees bent with the hot breaths of the winds, and the blue skies were obliterated, leaving the sun a shadowy outline in the sky. Hot from hell, the new winds howled as they blew. They carried the chaff from the earth up into the air, bending and snapping the hollow reeds and the desiccated trees. The winds jerked the air-borne insects into crazy flights and scattered the struggling birds flying in formation. It roared and it swelled, blowing its devastating breath of destruction everywhere. It howled, rubbing dry thing against dry thing. It lifted up everything in its path; all things that lay dead upon the earth were lifted up and disintegrated by the death-driven winds. They came inexorably over the land, carrying all things closer and closer towards the darkened horizon, tugging the weakened bodies towards the edge. All that could resist, resisted. The rest perished.

The sun continued its circuit, rising above the land in the morning and sinking, spent, every evening. It blazed cruelly, unmoved by the force of the earth's winds. But the winds blew and tugged until our lungs seemed to swell with breathlessness. Life was unbearable; not for even one more day could we take this devastation! Around us were gasping, starving, weakened people. Consumed with rage and terror, they saw the far clouds gather soundlessly, darkening, their great shadows looming ominous upon the desiccated earth. The winds stopped. For a timeless moment all was still.

And then, from across the barren stillness came the first howling rent of thunder.

The sky tore apart! Roaring orgiastically through the clouds, the sky tore open, lighting the earth with flashes of white lightning. The earth and sky shuddered together, and in a streak of white light the heavens poured down their blessed rains.

2 *Monsoon*

WITHIN MOMENTS THE LAND WAS FLOODED. Pounded upon and ravished, the earth received its torrential burden as the clouds opened and their rain cleaved through the heavy smog, beating down upon the earth's dust. The dust was churned immediately into percolating mud, which pressed against the thirsting earth and penetrated deeper and deeper towards the firm bedrock beneath, the surface of dust yielding, yielding. The water gushed, steaming against the hot ground and pouring into the dry gullies. The tanks and the ponds filled slowly, and the bleached beds of the rivers darkened with wetness.

Black thunderheads shrieked across the sky wrenching loose their boiling rain into the dry wells and the mud-cracked fields. The earth hissed as the torrents drenched it, sucking the seething waters towards the roots and seeds which lay dormant beneath its surface. Thirstily were the first rains received, as they washed through the air above, releasing it from the choking dust.

Beneath the mud the rich roots swelled and the seeds burst their softened shells; the monsoon earth steamed muskily, filling the pregnant air with a bittersweet musk that clung, like perfume, to one's skin. We breathed it in with longing and nostalgia and felt the aching desires of spring. Spring—the monsoon—had come to the North Indian plains.

The grasses sprung green and rustled with the birds that wriggled delightedly through their wetness; the young shoots swelled into petaled cuplets, which carried the weight of the fresh dew. Sprouts of *buleria* blossomed and grew waxy, and the *rat rani* vines twined about old stalks and new stalks, budding into flower at each sunrise, and the fields were green and dotted with colored flowers. Yellow acacia and red bougainvillea, hair-filled poppies and white *motia*, all bloomed and faded, giving way to the next and the next and the next.

The world seemed to swarm suddenly with creatures up from sleep, flying and buzzing and calling. They crowded the budding bushes and croaked at the puddle edges, wings in motion and eyes and mouths bulging, swallowing bugs too big for their throats. The hollow-sided beasts tore, famished, at the fragrant grasses, their heads against the earth for days on end, and the birds chased in raucous mating, their colored plumage flashing against the greens and blues of the monsoon world.

And back to this fragrant, enormous world came all the people who had escaped at the beginning of the long, hot summer. They returned from the mountains and the seacoasts; they emerged from tightly curtained bungalows and called to each other across the lanes. Loose-haired women in yellow saris gossiped on the lawns, and the children came out, shining plaits flying and high-pitched laughter ringing as they ran splashing through the puddles. The school gongs clanged, and the wayside temples were piled with offerings of food in thanks. It would be a good monsoon; the first rains were auspicious.

It was a good time. Each moment seemed new, like a soap-bubble which opened and then burst with a pop into the next. David and I felt giddy, romping like the children, through the gurgling puddles and laughing delightedly at almost anything that came up; everything was funny. We came towards each other with a rush of gladness, like the tendrils of creeping vines that shot, like young green snakes, along the ground. We felt ungrounded and silly. It was all so simple—one had only to live!

We stood one evening on the lane outside our bungalow chatting with Mira and Vikram, our close friends who had been gone all summer. Mira was a nurse at the campus hospital and was asking me about the events of the summer on the campus when Chakravorty came puffing up the lane, his body swaying heavily on the bicycle seat as he pedaled.

"You must come to my party!" he called out with effort, his legs pumping up and down on the pedals as he continued past us. "All of you! All!" He waved one hand magnanimously around and nearly toppled over, but obviously he had no intention of stopping.

Mira shook her head as if to say, he's still the same Chakravorty; and we all ran after him, shouting, "When?" The four of us were laughing as we caught up with him, and the bicycle teetered and came to a halt as Chakravorty stepped down and looked at us perplexed and cross that we had stopped him. "When my daughter arrives," he replied in a voice that implied "of course."

"When is that?" we all repeated at once, and then giggled.

He turned to us in exasperation as his toe fumbled for the pedal, and with an expostulation of breath, declared, "Saturday—at seven," as if incredulous that we should not know. And shifting his weight he pulled the bicycle forward on one pedal and plunked himself square on the seat, taking off again down the wet gravel path.

On the evening of the party the air was soft and fragrant, and the path steamed pleasantly beneath our feet as we made our way towards Chakravorty's house. The songs and scrapings of a thousand insects chirruped about us, and the evening sun was bowing amidst red and golden rays at the cloud-horizon before us. David raised his sandalwood cane towards the cloud formations, pointing out the subtle green sky behind us and the masses of puffed pink clouds to our right. We stopped for a moment and watched as the colors merged and changed like a kaleidoscope, wisps of henna deepening the edge of the green while the cloud masses moved into newer forms before our eyes. I readjusted the *pallou* of my new silk sari over my shoulder, enjoying the soft rustle as it slipped immediately down my arm again. Linking my arm through David's, we continued slowly down the paths, watching the sky all the time and pointing out to each other in murmurs.

"See the white owl?"

"Hm-n."

"Weaver bird's nest. Must be eggs in there."

"Mm-n."

When we got to the Chakravorty's, the sun was still slipping through the cushion of colored clouds at the edge of the plains, and Chakravorty was out on his mat-spread lawn, completing his evening yoga before greeting the guests who were slowly arriving from all corners of the campus. He seemed oblivious of the crowd gathering around him as he arched his back slowly, pointing his belly directly towards the streaming sunset. He held the position with eyes closed and then with a grunt shifted forward, touching his toes with the ends of his fingers and gasping in short, belabored breaths. The sun drifted closer and closer to the earth, sending wafts of yellow light, which then rose from the land to meet it. The light grew orange and then fire red, growing brighter and brighter as the sun descended, finally burning the edge in a stripe of searing flame as the last arc of the sun disappeared beneath the horizon. A flash of green, and then a pulsing glow which pulled at the cushion of darkness to close the breach between the heaven and the earth. And it was night.

The company was silent, and Chakravorty completed the last posture of his sun worship. He stood with palms together before his face, his eyes squinting appraisingly at the sunset.

Speaking slowly and authoritatively, he said, "In Bengal it is even better than that."

The servants stood together on the veranda, watching the guests arrive, and when Chakravorty completed his evening worship Ram Dulare approached him with a burning stick of incense and then retreated into the house towards the kitchen. Shanti followed him, slipping on bare feet across the veranda, her faded purple sari swishing about her ankles, and she emerged shortly carrying a lighted *hookah* filled with burning coals, which she placed in the center of the lawn alongside a knot of people.

"Ahh-h!" exclaimed Vikram, kneeling down beside the mouth stem of the water pipe. "Chakravorty thinks of everything!" He drew deeply upon the *hookah,* setting the water to burbling, and exhaled with a look of deep satisfaction. "Excellent," he sighed with satisfaction, handing the pipe stem over to David, who stood above him. "Excellent!"

As people arrived they greeted each other with loud cries and polite kisses, glad to find each other again after the long summer. Everyone talked at once, exchanging news of the summer and the children, the political situation and the rising prices, the threat of floods in the north and the threat of drought in the south. Mrs. Chakravorty, flushed and excited, bustled from one chatting group to another, herding her teen-aged daughter before her and introducing her to everyone she could interrupt, with especial persistence at the young Bengali students.

"This is my daughter Rumi," she would say, framing her stocky daughter with her proud arms. "Rumi, this is Ashok Ghosh, the boy in Physics who won the prize I wrote you about. His family is the Ghosh from Tollygange." Her eyes would flash signals to her daughter, at which Rumi would smile obediently at the guest, and then look down at her painted fingernails and examine them with concentration.

Vera walked carefully across the lawn, holding onto the silk of her light blue sari, which kept slipping down to her waist. She glanced down at her bare midriff again and again, as if uneasy at its exposed whiteness, and covered it over with the edge of her sari as best she could. Balancing a drink in her free hand she smiled uncomfortably at Mira and me as she approached us, hugging her elbows to her sides to keep her sari from slipping farther.

"*Namaste,* Vera," said Mira with a warm twinkle. "You need an extra tuck. Come inside and I shall help you."

Mira was warm, plump, and bosomy, and was probably the only woman on campus who could have offered help to Vera without offending her.

"No, no, I'm all right," Vera claimed, adjusting her arms and drink carefully.

"Mira has just been telling me about her summer in Gujarat with her family," I told Vera. "There is a Maternal Care Clinic in Baroda which sounds like a marvelous set-up for around here." I turned to Mira, and she began enthusiastically to tell Vera her ideas for starting a clinic on the campus.

Ram Dulare padded up to us with a trayful of fried snacks, responding to our greeting with a submissive bow, and when he shuffled off we told Mira about the summer's events. Mira clucked, her motherly face downcast as we added that Shanti's dowry had been used up in the process.

The moon had risen, looming suddenly yellow above us, and Shanti stepped off the veranda carrying a bowl of hot coals, her silver nose-ring reflecting their light. She slipped unobtrusively to the bubbling *hookah* where she dumped them in gingerly and glanced up at the moon before retreating into the house to continue with the preparations for dinner.

The fireflies flitted through the darkening evening, jabbing light sparks through the swelling perfume of the night-blooming jasmine. Light breezes carried bursts of talk and laughter from one group to another, and the party settled into a humming course.

"Hey, Chakravorty!" somebody called from across the lawn. "What was it like around here all summer? It is your first time remaining in station, isn't it?"

Chakravorty made a socially wry face and winking to his companions retorted, "It was dull and hot. You think this place should change just because I stay around?"

Ram Dulare held a tray of crisp *pappadum* wafers towards a cluster of people, and after they helped themselves he moved on to another group. Ganesh came onto the veranda and signaled to his father; Ram Dulare nodded and came to me, handing me the last two *pappadums* and scurrying to the veranda with his empty tray. As he and Ganesh lugged a long wooden table onto the veranda, Shanti poked her head out the door and let her eyes roam over the assembled guests before she was put to work at carrying the heaping platters of food to the table. For the next fifteen minutes all three were occupied in bringing food in bowls and dishes from the kitchen to the veranda.

Pungent aromas of mixed spices wafted towards us on the lawn as the *pullaos* and curries and *dhals* appeared and were set down upon the table. Mrs. Chakravorty officiated, supervising the setting down of the wheaten *puri* and chutneys and curds and pickles and the endless curries. With her fingers knotted nervously at her midriff, she jerked her flushed face up and down the table critically, goading Shanti to move faster, ordering Ram Dulare with impatience.

"Move, move! They will all starve waiting for you!" Shanti lowered her eyes and hunching her back, ran.

Finally, the food was all out, and in a voice thick with anticipation, Mrs. Chakravorty announced to her guests, "Now you may come! Come now! Come now!" Sweeping towards us with outstretched arms she herded us up to the serving table.

The heaping platters were continually replenished as Ram Dulare, dripping with perspiration, ran to and fro from the huge pots in the kitchen to the serving dishes on the veranda. We filled our plates, whispering to Ram Dulare as we passed him, "It looks perfect, Ram Dulare."

"That is good *sahib, mem sahib,*" he bowed with dignity.

David and I sat on a mat and dipped our fingers into the steaming mounds of curry and rice, licking the sticky food off our hands. The spices stung my palate and brought tears to my eyes, and I bit into a crisp, sweet onion to soothe my burning throat. Ram Dulare saw me cough, and he disappeared inside, bringing out with him a glass of water for me.

"Boiled, *mem sahib,*" he announced, standing stiff and proper in his white party uniform. "You can drink it."

"Thank you, Ram Dulare," I said, reaching for the glass, touched that he had thought of boiling up water for us. The glass was almost too hot to hold, but I let it burn my fingers until Ram Dulare had disappeared into the doorway of the house, and then I gingerly put it down before collapsing into laughter. David picked up the glass to see what was so funny, and he immediately dropped it, nursing his fingers and laughing with me.

"Boiled water!" we said together through our giggles.

Shanti came out with veiled eyes, and again crept through the groups of people who were seated and standing about the garden; glancing about furtively, she tossed three more live coals onto the bubbling *hookah*. Then, stacking the crusted plates that were piled beneath the table where the guests had left them, she carried a pile back into the kitchen for washing, and then returned for more. My palate had become accustomed to the sharp sting of the chili, and I finished the rest of my dinner with relish, licking my fingers clean after the meal like a contented cat. Mrs. Chakravorty planted herself in front of each of her guests, urging us to take more, pouting coyly that we would insult her if we refused.

"It was wonderful, really," I protested, patting my bare midriff to show her how full I was.

"Our Bengali cooking, you do not like it too well, you hardly took anything!" she insisted, her head tilted coyly at David and me.

"Madam," David announced gallantly, "To prove my appreciation, I will help myself to more." And with a formal bow to her, and a wink at me, he followed her to the table on the veranda.

Finally, the food was cleared away and the company sprawled lazily about on the mats, smoking on the water pipe and chewing on the betel nut that Chakravorty passed around. The talk had drifted into a comfortable murmur, and the air was a mingled breath of perfumed smoke, jasmine, and scented *charras* leaf. People relaxed and stretched out, leaning on their elbows and laughing softly at the jokes that were passing languorously from one to the other. Venkataraman beat out a quiet rhythm on the seat of a hard, wooden stool, and soon toes and fingers were snapping and moving with the pulsing beat. Vikram, leaning on Mira's legs beside us, took up the rhythm and beat it out against his thighs, and his eyelids fluttered contentedly when somebody's voice rose into a song. We all hummed along, laughing softly with pleasure when we came to the end of the song.

"Mira, sing for us!"

Mira's renditions of love songs from her native Gujarat were famous on the campus, and a gathering was never complete unless Mira had sung, in her sweet warbling voice, one of those songs that told of the night and of love.

She smiled shyly across at us and whispered, "Should I?"

"Please, Mira, do *'Gheri Gheri.'* " I coaxed. "We haven't heard it all summer."

Mira blushed and looked back at her husband Vikram, who had already grabbed the wooden stool from Venkataraman and was drumming vigorously upon its seat. Chakravorty bustled inside and reappeared with a pair of *tabla* drums, which were

reached for by many hands, and Mira settled herself on the mat
and patting out a rhythm in her lap, began her song.

It was a song of love—of a night fragrant with the night-
blooming jasmine and of a young girl entreating her lover to
play his flute quietly, secretly, so that his sweet music might
enter her dreams.

> Come! O Form of the formless
> Come in the guise of dreamy music
> And let my heart glow with you.

The gathering swayed and hummed with her.

> *Gheri gheri raatarani, foramati dali dali*
> *Mara haiya naa ughade dwar—Ahhhh.*

When her song was finished, she made a small gesture with
folded hands before her face and smiled at the others. We
begged for another, and Mira sang another. And then Venkataraman's wife sang a song from Madras, and Chakravorty ran inside
to bring out some hard wooden bowls to be used for drumming.
Soon the garden pulsed with rhythm and voices, and a great deal
of confusion and laughter between songs. Ganesh and Shanti
squatted in the shadows of the veranda, listening, their eyes
glowing in the dark. Ram Dulare had disappeared to his room
before having to clean up after the guests had left, and Padma
had not been seen all evening. Presumably she was asleep in the
back.

The evening wore on and the moon rose higher into the sky,
growing whiter and more distant as it climbed. We sang and we
rested, we smoked and we chewed the intoxicating betel nut.
Vera had been seated primly nearby, but her head began to nod,
and the drape of her sari had slipped off her shoulder.

"I think I've had too much of this," she declared when she
felt my eyes on her, holding her glass aloft. I laughed, and she
defiantly took another sip, saying, "There!"

Vikram turned to her and asked, "What about an American song from you three?"

Vera tittered. "Me? Sing?"

"Of course!" agreed Mira, "an American song! Please give us a song."

"What shall we sing, Vera?" I asked, shrugging, able to think of nothing but "I've Been Working on the Railroad."

" 'I've Been Working on the Railroad,' " Vera announced without hesitation. "Yes, I know that song." For the second time I was astounded by how close I felt to Vera.

We started our song on different pitches, and amidst giggles, began again. It was hard to sing without laughing, and finally in the refrain, "Fee, fi, fiddly-i-o," Vera sputtered and dropped the drink from her hand, laughing with embarrassment and her eyes running with tears, the end of her sari down around her waist. The company finished the song for us, "Strummin' on the old banjo," and everyone applauded. Shanti sat hidden in the corner of the veranda, watching Vera out of cat-sharp eyes, her expression never changing. While everyone begged Chakravorty to sing, Shanti rose and slipped silently off the veranda into the dark shadows by the side of the house and did not return.

"A Tagore song!" everyone had coaxed Chakravorty. "Sing us a Tagore song."

The songs of Tagore were beautiful and were known to every Bengali the way that Mother Goose is known to everyone brought up in America. Chakravorty and his wife argued in rapid Bengali over which song to sing. Rumi, their daughter, joined in, suggesting this song or that song, each of which was rejected before they reached their decision. Finally, Chakravorty faced his guests, and with eyes growing moist he began to sing. It was a prayer that he sang, an offering to God. He intoned the repeated notes.

Ahguner, parashmana chhaon pranay, eh jibone
punna kawro, eh jibone punna kawro, eh jibone
punna kawro . . .

His voice rose pleadingly with the melody as it lifted into the
higher registers of the next line.

> Lord, touch me with the touchstone of fire
> And make this life holy.
> My body is the lamp of fire for your temple . . .

Mrs. Chakravorty joined him, her voice cracking at first but
then growing stronger, and to their duet was added the young
voice of their daughter.

> *Nishidin ahloke sheekha jolook pranay* . . .
>
> Let the flame of my song burn day and night
> Upon the darkness. Your touch lights new and
> endless stars into the darkness all night long.
> Make that darkness disappear from my eyes;
> Spark your light into that darkness so that
> All my pain will burn upwards towards Heaven.

Tears coursed down Chakravorty's face, and stretching out his
big arms he pressed his wife and daughter to his sides. His voice
faltered, and he buried his head in Rumi's neck and allowed his
wife and guests to complete the last refrain of his song without
him.

The days and weeks passed in calm succession. The air was
filled with the tropical tangle of wild greenery and with the
hoarse cries of farmers straining behind their oxen in the muddy
fields. With the steaming sunrises came the flocks of new birds
across the fields to settle in the dense foliage of the mango trees;
and with the clouds and rainbows of the sunsets they clamored
back again from where they had come. The days were alternately
fresh and humid, wild cloudbursts followed by balmy nights;
swelling humidity followed by crystal rains.

We all went back to our work, and life settled again into a
routine. Each morning David went off to the Institute to teach

his classes and conduct his research in the laboratory, and each morning I went out into the surrounding villages and through the servants' quarters with my bag full of bandages and aspirins.

Ganesh had been given Rudra's former job at the Venkataraman's house, and Ram Dulare continued on at the Chakravorty's, putting on his starched cap every morning and cooking up the Bengal curries that the Chakravortys ate three times a day. Shanti remained aloof, keeping house for her father and going once a day to the market in the village for a bunch of radishes or a handful of grain, her head high and her face stony. Only Padma could be seen around the campus, her sari hitched high in front and her hands folded on the ridge of her belly, wandering slowly across the gardens and through the paths, her small face blank and wistful.

One night we were awakened from sleep by a harsh tapping on the panes of our bedroom window. The taps accompanied a husky entreaty, *"Mem sahib—mem sahib!"*

The sounds entered my sleep and were dispelled by my dream, but the noises persisted. *"Mem sahib—mem sahib!"*

I sat up and saw Shanti peering through the opening in the bedroom curtains, her forehead furrowed and her eyes worried.

"Mem sahib, you must come!" she pleaded, and as I slipped into my robe, she darted around to the front door to be let in.

"The baby," she explained anxiously, covering her head apologetically and looking up at me with urgent eyes.

"How long have the pains been coming?" I asked, slipping out of my robe and into a dress right there in the darkened hall.

"Ram Dulare said I should not come until morning, but I know it cannot wait that long," Shanti apologized, watching with fascination as I buckled my belt and ran a brush through my hair. "Since the evening after dinner she has been having pains."

I nodded and went into the kitchen to gather up my delivery

equipment: a cardboard box filled with newspapers and a sterile kit filled with scissors, shoelaces, and a syringe.

David called from the bedroom, "Hey, what's going on out there?" His voice was husky and bewildered, and Shanti shot me a questioning look.

"It's all right," I called back, going in to him before leaving. "Padma's baby is ready and Shanti just came in to call me over." His eyes blinked a few times and then he turned over, slipping back down into sleep, as I left. Handing Shanti the cardboard box, I first checked the time—it was 4 o'clock in the morning— piled the rest in my arms and closed the door behind us, stepping out into the silent, nighttime street.

The air was soft and humid, silent except for the haunting calls of the night owls that watched us with iridescent eyes from the branches of the trees. Dew dripped from the bushes, and a mist lay suspended in the beam of light from the street lamps, making the nighttime mission even more secretive than it would have been in the day. We passed Mira's house, and I remembered that she had offered to assist me at this delivery, but after a moment of deliberation, decided not to wake her.

"Is Padma very uncomfortable, do you think?" I asked Shanti as we stepped around puddles, both our arms filled with bags and boxes. Shanti looked at me appraisingly before remarking with a derisive curl of her lips, "Oh, she has been screaming that she is going to die."

Poor Padma, I thought. She is so young for all that has happened to her. I said out loud, "She must be very frightened. It is very hard for her, because she has no mother or sisters to help her." I waited for Shanti to concede to that, but she shrugged and said nothing.

"It is very hard to be a widow in your country," I continued, trying to soften Shanti into some empathy for Padma. "And to be a widow so young, is very hard."

Shanti began to speak, but then held her tongue.

"No?" I urged.

Finally, after great hesitation, she blurted out, "If she had not done something evil to deserve being a widow, then she would not be a widow." She paused and added in a bitter undertone, "and my brother would still be alive."

We continued walking in silence, and I added to myself, "And you would be married to your boy from Lucknow."

We arrived at Chakravorty's and tiptoed down the brick path alongside the house to the quarters in the back. Again I was coming to that same place.

Ram Dulare and Ganesh met us at the top of the path, both disheveled and sleepy-eyed, both kneeling to touch my feet in gratitude for coming. I tried to be cheerful and whispered to them, "Will we have a boy or a girl?" They looked at each other and shrugged, taking my question seriously.

"Ram Dulare," I said, "you must sleep." He nodded obediently and watched as Ganesh dragged his *charpoy* to a plot that lay fallow at the other end of the garden, and bowing to me, he went to it, lay down, and fell asleep.

"Ganesh," I ordered, looking about me and trying to organize the order of events in my head, "make me a fire out here, and I want a kettle of water to boil."

"Yes, *mem sahib*," he replied with alacrity, hiding from me the soggy dung cake he picked from the bottom of the fuel pile.

I immediately counted on doing without sterile water, and said to Shanti, "I want clean cloths, and please let me examine Padma alone until I call for you."

"Yes, *mem sahib*," replied Shanti, bowing.

The sickle moon had disappeared behind a filmy cloud, making an eerie smudge of light in one corner of the sky, and after taking a deep breath of the night air, I picked up the cardboard box with all the equipment and stepped into the room.

Except for the one feeble lightbulb, the room was deep in shadows. The *charpoy* lay in the far corner, and upon it Padma was tossing and moaning, her breath coming in surprised gasps and her hair wild about her head. She seemed so tiny, covered in that ragged wisp of a sari, and the burden of her belly was so large for her body.

"*Namaste,* Padma," I said softly, announcing my presence as I put down the box in the corner by the tap. "How goes it?" Padma merely groaned and twisted, turning her head towards me but not attempting a response. I came close and stood by the *charpoy,* looking down. She was in the midst of a contraction, and she gnashed her teeth and stared up at me accusingly. I bent over her and brushed the hair from her face, crooning soothingly to her before placing a hand upon her belly. She began to protest, but bit her lip and lay back, exhausted. I wondered how much she understood of what was happening to her, and as I ran my fingers across her back, I told her reassuringly that her baby had to come out, and this was his way of letting her know that he was ready, and that by the time the sun was high in the sky she would have a baby all her own. She looked at me mistrustingly, but she listened, and when I rose to prepare the room for the delivery, she held out her hand to call me back.

She sat up, shifting her ungainly weight, her features tensing in misery. Slowly, she heaved herself off the cot and lowered her body into a squatting position on the floor. I came back to her and rubbed her back, timing the contraction on my wrist watch.

"Very good," I announced cheerfully. She looked up at me with hurt eyes and said nothing. I squatted down to her level and asked, "Will you let me examine you so I will know how soon the baby will be born?"

She looked reluctant, but pulled herself up and swayed onto the *charpoy,* closing her eyes in pain as she moved. Lying down, she hitched her sari sloppily above her hips, and opened eyes which did not see out. The light was bad, and I went to the window and opened it. Ganesh was there immediately, anxious but keeping his head turned the other way so as not to see in.

"It's fine," I said reassuringly. "I just needed some light."

Padma shivered when I placed my cold stethoscope upon her belly to listen for the baby's heartbeats, and her thighs began uncontrollably to tremble. Her brown flesh goose-pimpled, and I murmured "good" at hearing the strong, regular beats of the baby's heart.

Suddenly she clamped her legs together and grimaced, seizing my arms with icy fingers and clinging to me. She whimpered piteously and hung desperately onto me. I timed the contraction and rubbed her cold hands until it subsided. "Good," I said again, and waited until she lay back and released her hold on me before going out to call Shanti.

The clouds were scudding across the sickle moon, revealing it and hiding it as they moved.

"Shanti," I called in a loud whisper, not seeing her anywhere. "Shanti!"

A rustle, and Shanti rose from her flower-pot altar, where she was performing her prayers, tossing grains of rice and jasmine flower and water onto the sacred river stones.

"I was saying prayer to my God," she said, almost apologetically. She smiled shyly, rubbing her hands against her thighs to dry them. *"Mem sahib,"* she began hesitantly.

"Yes?"

"When Rudra was sick, I prayed for Rudra."

"Yes, Shanti," I replied, touched.

"And when you said you had no babies, I prayed that you would have babies."

I stopped, and taking her hand, asked, "Are you praying now for Padma and Rudra's baby?"

She stared at me curiously. "No," she said slowly, "I am praying for God to bring me a husband."

Shanti and I stepped back into the room as Padma relaxed from the strain of her last contraction. Her forehead was damp

with perspiration, and the sinews in her neck stood out. Shanti
held the flashlight as I examined Padma's cervix, finding that she
was almost two fingers dilated.

"I think we won't have to wait much longer," I announced,
looking down at my watch. It was a bit after five in the morning,
and I guessed that the baby would come within the next two
hours. "We'd better get the room ready," I told Shanti, pointing
to the cardboard box in the corner by the tap, for her to bring
me.

First I pulled the *charpoy,* with Padma still on it, to the center
of the room, where I could make use of whatever small light
shone through the window. The darkness was breaking up
slowly into gray, and by the time the baby came we would probably have some sunlight. Then I unfolded the sheaf of newspapers from the cardboard box and spread them all over the room,
saving the thickest pile for padding under Padma's body. Shanti
looked at the pictures in the newspaper as she lay the sheets all
around the room, and appeared mystified when I asked her to
help me tug open the hemp strings of the *charpoy* where Padma's
feet were. I placed the empty carton under the foot of the bed
and showed her that if we made an opening in the strings all the
drippings from the birth would fall directly into the box and not
foul the floor. Shanti was impressed, but had never seen any such
precautions taken before. In the villages childbirths were handled
by the barbers' wives, who either caught the baby as it emerged
or reached in with bare hands to get it if it didn't emerge. Other
than that, childbirth was unclean and ritually polluted, and anybody who had contact with a woman in labor or a just-born in-
fant was immediately contaminated.

Padma was clutching at her bent knees, her knuckles clenched
white and her teeth grinding as the wave of her pain progressed.
I timed the contraction, wishing I could somehow make it easier
for her, sponging her brow with a warm, wet cloth as she tossed
her head from side to side. There was still time to go.

I motioned to Shanti to stay by Padma and rub her back, and I went to lay out my simple instruments for the delivery: one pair of sterile rubber gloves, one pair of white shoelaces for tying the umbilical cord, a bandage scissors for cutting the cord, and a syringe of Ergonovine to be used in the event of postpartum bleeding.

I called out the window to Ganesh, "Did you get a fire going?"

He appeared suddenly, his face turned the other way and whispered hoarsely, "I'm still trying, *mem sahib* . . ."

Oh, well, I thought resignedly, at least we'll have some hot water for tea after the baby is born.

Padma was grabbing restlessly at her ankles, clutching at the sides of the *charpoy* and trying to get up. I bent down to help her, but then her face grimaced and she lay back helpless, straining and grunting through clenched teeth as her womb contracted strongly. Writhing, she tossed more and more violently, ending the long pain with an involuntary scream. She lay panting, looking up at me with pleading intensity, and I sponged her neck, kneading her belly gently with my hand to help her relax for the next contraction. As it came on she stared up, panic-stricken, and held onto me. Her mouth was edged with dry spittle, and her low moan became a series of sharp grunts as she wept, helpless and beaten by the intensity of pain within her. I couldn't help but remember Rudra writhing on this same *charpoy,* but I dispelled the image as a long wail escaped from Padma's throat, and folding her hands in agitated prayer above her face, she cried. "Rama! Rama! Please, Rama, save me!" She swallowed hard, her face distorted with panic. "Aiyee, Rama-aa!"

The contraction subsided and she lay still. There was still a while to go before I would hear that final, searing cry that marked the stage of crowning. I could hear Ganesh pacing nervously outside and saw the sky growing lighter and lighter as the sun began to rise over the plains in the east. I poked my head out

the window and saw Ganesh and greeted Ram Dulare, who had
gotten up and was washing his head at the outside tap. A knot of
servant women had gathered and were standing about outside the
room, their babies suckling at their breasts or straddled upon
their hips.

"*Hai, mem sahib,*" they called, coming forward.

"Morning!" I greeted them, "no baby yet." I rubbed my eyes
sleepily, and yawning, called to Ram Dulare, "It's all right, the
baby will be soon." The kettle was blackening over a hissing
mound of cow dung, and I asked, "Could you bring it inside and
boil the water on Chakravorty's stove now? I don't think they'd
mind."

I turned back into the room as Padma started in terrified anticipation of the next contraction. I took a clean cloth from Shanti
and held it under the perineum to catch the oozing mucous,
stroking Padma's trembling thighs and watching for signs of
progress at the opening. Suddenly Padma clamped her legs together, screaming in pain. I motioned to Shanti to hold Padma's
knees apart; with a look of annoyance, Shanti held her legs as
Padma squirmed against Shanti, shrieking and trying to snatch at
the ball of pain between her legs. Shanti looked at me for approval and then flung Padma's arms up and sat on them, pinning
them against the *charpoy.*

Padma arched in fury, howling desperately from deep in her
throat. "Aiyeeee! Rama-aa! I am going to die!" Her eyes stared
wildly from her darkening face, and with an orgiastic shriek—
that crowning howl which meant that the baby was about to be
born—she screamed, "I am going to die!"

Poised over the perineal opening of her body I could see a
black, ridged head pushing against the straining pink flesh
beyond the opening. The head retreated slightly, molding backwards amidst bubbles of blood and mucous. Again the womb
contracted and the baby's head squeezed towards the gaping
opening, spreading it wider and wider. Padma arched and yelled,

and again the baby's head retreated into the warm flesh of the birth canal. Straining with all her might, Padma choked as she bore down with the next contraction, and the black head shot forward, stretching the perineal skin to a transparent whiteness. The opening bulged black, and for a moment, all hung suspended. Just as the head would have retreated again into the warm safety of its mother, it burst through into the air, with a loud *squlch*. The baby's head was born!

"Hello!" I cried involuntarily. There between the outstretched brown thighs of its young mother lay a tiny human face! Little lips pouted beneath still nostrils and puffy eyelids curled with wet eyelashes. The emerging head, with its glistening black hair, I had come to expect during the last stage of childbirth, but the face, with its tiny, perfect features still always took me by surprise.

"Hello," I breathed again in excitement, cradling the little head in my gloved hands and turning it gently towards Padma's right thigh. With the next contraction I eased out first one shoulder and then the other, and then held the tiny buttocks as they came dripping out, followed by little legs and flailing arms. The baby was born!

"It's a boy!" I croaked, calling first in English and then in French before I finally got it out in Hindi. "A boy!" My voice was grainy with excitement, and I looked happily around at Shanti, who was busy unfolding cloths to wrap the baby in. "A boy!" I held up the baby to Padma, but she lay still and mortified, her face turned towards the wall and her eyes withdrawn from us.

I grasped the baby's ankles and supported his slippery body with my other arm. The twisted cord stretched purple between him and Padma, and with a wet gurgle he sucked in his first breath and squalled out his first, hot cry into the air. I laughed and yawned in excitement, holding him out at arm's length to get a better look at him. The rising sun sent a shaft of bright light into the dark corners of the room, and I held him up towards the corner, into the white light of the morning sun, grasping his slippery body firmly and squinting against the unaccustomed brightness. The light flashed in my eyes and I blinked, rubbing my eyes against my shoulder and yawning uncontrollably. But a pulsing flash of whiteness seemed to be coming from the corner of the room, and hugging the baby to me I shook my head to clear the vision. The baby breathed warmly in my arms, and above his head I could almost swear to be seeing a man—no —but yes, there in the corner it was as if a dark man swathed in dead-white cloths was sitting and looking at us. A dark, bald head and heavy-lidded eyes, and the rest was this blinding whiteness.

The hairs on my arms stood up, and I shook my head to dispel the vision of fatigue. But I lifted my eyes again to the corner, and unmistakably, something was sitting there, which hurt my eyes to look at.

No! My heart contracted strangely, and I clung to the warm wetness of the baby, but I could not take my eyes from the white blur that burned out at me from the corner of the room.

"What is it?" Shanti asked uneasily, following my stare into the corner of the room.

"Do you see something—uh—white?" I asked shakily.

"Just the sunlight," she answered slowly, looking at me curiously.

"I must just be tired," I mumbled, not knowing if I was just tired or not, but still afraid to look up again into the corner. Busying myself with the baby, I put him down upon the *charpoy* next to his mother and tied the cord carefully with two shoelaces before cutting through it to separate them. Wrapping him in a clean cloth, I helped to deliver the afterbirth, which slipped out easily, and then gathered up all the newspapers and cloths from the birth, stuffed them into the soiled carton beneath the cot, and took another happy look at the peacefully sleeping newborn.

Next to do was to tell Ram Dulare and Ganesh that all was
well, and then I could go home and get some sleep.

My head was bent over the cot, and my breath caught when it
came to straightening to leave the room, but I shot one quick
look of trepidation into the corner of the room and for a moment
seemed to see a white-shrouded figure, but I turned quickly and
stumbled out the door as fast as I could, calling back to Shanti,
"I'll come back tonight." I ran into the sunshine to tell the men
in the kitchen that it was a boy.

The sun glistened off every drop of dew that hung from leaf
and ledge. Blinking, I leaned for a moment against the doorpost
when the knot of servant women who had been waiting outside
began to approach.

"*Hai, mem sahib,*" they called, turning to each other and titter-
ing.

"It's a boy! A big, healthy boy," I announced, moving off towards the house. But the women were not satisfied. They followed me closely, careful not to touch me in my bloody apron
and unwashed hands, holding their babies out to me and sticking
out sore lips and limbs for me to see.

"*Mem sahib—mem sahib,*" they all whined at me, "look at the
baba, how sick—my skin, it's coming off—come see my husband,
he is in bed and cannot move—*mem sahib, mem sahib . . .*" I
stopped, dazed.

"What?" I asked, dumb with weariness. The babble started up
again, louder and more persistent. Arms were thrust in my face,
staring babies with running sores were shoved at me, all the
while accompanied by strident whines. I felt trapped and broke
away from them at a run, my head in a confusion of helplessness.

Bursting through the kitchen door I found Ram Dulare and
Ganesh squatting together by the stove, their eyes wide with ex-
pectation and their fingers knotted over their knees. Ganesh was
dressed to go to work, and they both snapped to attention, saluting me smartly.

"Sit down," I told them, disappointed that they should still respond to me that way. "You have a boy—congratulations!" I
stepped forward with my hand outstretched, and instead of smiling proudly at the good luck of having a man-child, they both
turned gray and shrank away from me, huddling together and
looking furtively for a way out. Oh—it must be my apron, I reasoned, and with exaggerated gestures I untied my apron strings
and tossed the offending bit of cloth out the back door. I washed
my hands at the sink, scrubbing carefully before approaching
them again to offer my congratulations. Again both men shrank
from me, looking helplessly at each other and moving towards
the door with fear-stricken eyes. Ganesh paled, looking as if he'd
seen a ghost instead of just the woman who had delivered his sister-in-law's baby. But the taboos of ritual uncleanliness had been
instilled from birth, I thought, and the blood upon my hands
was threatening enough to make him run from me with that desperate stare of fear.

That desperate stare of fear! With a sudden shock I knew that
I had seen that expression on Ganesh's face before, and the time
I had seen it was when he had stared into the corner, transfixed
by something in the corner, alongside Rudra's bed at the hospital! Yes, Ganesh had seen something in the corner—now I suddenly remembered! Something that he could not take his eyes
from! Then perhaps my eyes had not deceived me—perhaps I
had seen something in the corner of that room—perhaps what I
had seen was what Ganesh had seen that night in the hospital in
the corner of the ward!

I had to know. My hands fell at my sides, and breathing heavily I stared at him.

"Ganesh," I began, stepping towards him, choking on his
name. He moved back away from me, his eyes darting towards
the doorway for a place to disappear to. I did not care if I was
frightening him, I had to know. My head was filled with anticipation and dread, but there was something that only Ganesh and

I knew about—or maybe not—and I had to know from him what it was that he had seen in the corner of that room!

"Yes, I thought I heard something going on in here!" squealed Mrs. Chakravorty as she entered the kitchen, her hair still disheveled from sleep and her sleeping sari limp and creased about her. "My dear, what brings you here at such an hour? You should still be in bed."

Ganesh stood with his back against the screen door, ready to flee, and without taking my eyes off him, I said shortly to her, "Padma's baby is born. It's a boy. Why don't you go have a look at him?"

"Later, later," she said solicitously, "but let me first take care of you. You must be exhausted." I brushed her aside with my hand, which she carefully and instinctively avoided, and still with my eyes on Ganesh, mumbled, "No, leave me be. I'm all right."

"You would say that," she persisted with a motherly laugh, "but I wouldn't dream of letting you leave here without some tea. Ram Dulare, make *mem sahib* a pot of tea!"

"No, please!" I turned to her for an instant, pleading, and in that instant Ganesh took his chance, and backing out the screen door, fled out of sight.

After almost an hour I finally escaped from Mrs. Chakravorty, having had to make pleasant conversation and watch Chakravorty eat his mammoth breakfast of flat bread and fish. I felt dizzy and nauseous by the time I reached home, still sticky and stale with the odors of the birth. Although it was only eight o'clock in the morning, by the time I reached home I felt as if I had been up a full day. Still surrounded by the aura of the birth, I was disconcerted to find David and Jagdish waiting for me with breakfast laid out on the table.

"Everything go all right?" David greeted me, putting his arm around my shoulder and kissing me lightly on the nose. I felt preoccupied, and my first impulse was to tell him everything, but

something checked me from speaking, and I answered, moving
out of his grasp. "Yeah. She had a boy, and it took a while, but
they're O.K. Do you mind if I bathe before I do anything else?"

"Sure," answered David.

"Umm," I mumbled, and shuffled off without another word to
the bathroom.

That evening I went again to Ram Dulare's quarters to check
on Padma and the baby. The sun was setting off in the west, and
my chest felt tight with nervousness as I walked across the lanes
towards the room where Padma lay. Ganesh would be outside,
probably working in his small garden, and tonight I had to try
and talk to him alone. I had no idea how to begin, but I had to
find out if he had seen what I thought I had seen. If he confessed
to having seen a man in the corner by Rudra's deathbed, then I
would know I had seen something in the room of Padma's delivery—and until I was certain, I could not say anything to David.
David would certainly be skeptical, and before I told him I had
to be absolutely sure.

When I arrived at the servants' compound Ganesh was squatting next to Shanti in the mud outside the door, fanning the fire
in the mud fireplace into flames. Shanti squinted against the
smoke; she was chopping onions and potatoes into a brass vessel,
which sat, sputtering, upon the *chula,* the fireplace. Ganesh rose
when he saw me and stood aside respectfully, looking away.

"*Namaste,*" I said, trying to keep my voice level. "How is
Padma doing?"

"*Tik hai,*" they both murmured politely, "she is inside."
Shanti stirred the curry mixture with a wooden spoon, sending a
sharp aroma of hot chili into the air above the cooking pot.

"I will go in to see her?" I said stupidly, not moving. They
both tilted their heads in acquiescence, but I stayed where I was,
uneasy and breathless.

I made a move towards Ganesh, and just as I was about to speak to him he put his head down and mumbled to Shanti that he would go to the garden and pick some coriander leaves. And turning, he left.

"You can just go inside, *mem sahib*," repeated Shanti, as I stood undecided as to whether or not to follow Ganesh. I had missed my chance, and taking a shaky breath, I stepped inside.

The room was dark and almost greenish with the single light bulb. It was empty except for the single *charpoy* upon which Padma and the baby lay. The corner—I checked with a quick glance—held nothing. Padma lay sleeping with her head turned away from the baby, and beneath the *charpoy* was a cast-iron pot filled with smoking dung. The black smoke billowed up slowly, filling the room with a stinking cloud that settled sootily upon everything in the room. The baby had been oiled and was covered with tiny flecks of black soot, which clung to his tiny, greased body. I coughed twice and rubbed at my stinging eyes. Padma did not stir.

"What's this?" I asked Shanti, poking my head out the door. "What did you put that in there for?"

She looked up from her cooking pot and replied, "We do that to keep the evil spirit away."

"But it is bad for the baby!" I insisted impatiently. "I can hardly breathe in there—how can he?" Shanti tilted her head and followed me in, and together we dragged the smoking pot out the door and brought it over to the flower-pot altar of mud and stones.

Padma did not stir as I checked the baby all over and listened to his heart tones. She did not stir when I read her blood pressure and took her temperature, and she lay submissive and limp when I checked her perineum to see if the blood flow was normal. I spoke encouragingly to her, but her eyes did not even blink. She'll be better tomorrow, I thought. The baby can do without food for another twenty-four hours. Her breasts were still small and soft. When he is ready for food, she'll be ready, I reasoned.

Ganesh was not there when I came out again. Disappointed, I said to Shanti, "I'll come back in the morning. They are both fine, but please don't put that dung pot back, no matter what."

Shanti rose to watch me go, bowing until I was gone; but when I returned the next morning the room was again filled with acrid smoke, the pot of dung sitting on the floor right beneath the baby. Ganesh was nowhere in sight, Ram Dulare was at work in the Chakravortys' kitchen, and Shanti had gone to the market for vegetables. I lugged the heavy pot to the doorstep and dragged it down the steps, dumping the hot dung and stamping out the embers with my feet and a bucket of water. It sizzled foully and I sneezed hard.

Padma still lay with her head turned towards the wall. Her eyes were open, but expressionless, and when I spoke to her, she did not respond. Her body lay tense and mortified, and when I tried to examine her she pulled roughly away from me and went rigid. I gathered the baby in my arms and held his warm little body against me. He had been rubbed with a paste of crushed mustard seed, and the pink of his flesh showed through the astringent yellow paste in little blotches. Crooning to him softly, I brought him round to where Padma could see him and knelt down beside her.

"He is beautiful," I said hopefully, suddenly distracted towards the corner. I looked again at the baby's face and again into the corner. It was as if it was the baby himself that I had seen in the corner—the baby as an old man. I shuddered and stood up. Placing the baby back onto the bed, I noticed an iron knife that had been laid just at his head, and with an exclamation I picked it up and tossed it into the corner near the tap.

For the next two days I came both in the morning and the evening. Padma never moved from her spot on the bed, never

turned to her new baby. Shanti explained that the mustard was
for keeping away the mosquitoes and that the smoking dung was
for keeping away the evil spirits. I acquiesced to the mustard but
dragged out, each morning and evening, the stinking pot of
smoking dung. Shanti explained that the iron knife at the baby's
head was to fight off the evil spirit, and each morning and each
evening I removed the sharp knife from its close proximity to
the baby, and each time I returned I found it back where it had
been. Padma lay mortified and Ganesh kept away. The one time
I did see him he looked at me with apprehension, as if to ask
why I was pursuing him. Perhaps he somehow sensed what I
wanted from him, and that made him retreat all the more. By
this time I was sure we shared an unfathomable bond, and this
bond was obsessing me.

On the third morning Mira came with me to Ram Dulare's
quarters. The baby had taken nothing but a few drops of goat's
milk sucked from a rag Shanti had held to his mouth, and
Padma, still rigid with the shock and mortification of the delivery, was growing hot with breast fever. Her breasts were firm
and engorged, and were dripping with excess milk that stained
the front of her sari. Mira knelt by her for a long time, talking
firmly and insistently to her. I stood by, impatient and restless,
stealing compulsive looks into the empty corner of the room,
holding the baby in my arms. Padma's eyelids flickered once or
twice, but other than that she would not respond.

Mira stood and shrugged to me, and with anger in her voice
remonstrated Padma, "Now get up and take care of your child.
You are a mother!" I placed the baby again by her side, and Mira
and I left the room.

I came again in the evening, hoping to see Ganesh there, but
he was obviously evading me, and I saw him slip around a corner
as I approached. Shanti greeted me with a smile, putting a finger
to her lips as I came up.

"She's doing it, *mem sahib*," she whispered, nodding towards

the closed room. I put my ear to the door and heard only a rising
and falling silence; but as I pulled away, there was the wet gurgle of an impatient cry. I smiled back at Shanti and tiptoed into
the room to find Padma leaning on one elbow, the baby nestled
alongside her, sucking hungrily on her full breast. She did not
look up when I entered, but kept her eyes focused on her baby's
sucking mouth, pressing her breast towards him with her fingers
when he lost firm hold of the nipple. Her dusty hair was still
tangled and her face still pale from shock, but the stark expression of her thin lips had softened, and her almond-shaped eyes
were dark and moist. She was bent over her child, the beginning
of a new smile rounding over her features as she experienced the
first delights of tenderness in her full breasts. She watched the
child suckle, not lifting her eyes from him, anxiously adoring
him like the madonna she had just become. She looked up once,
shyly and with an unsuppressed giggle. I caught the tears that
leapt into my throat and closed the door, standing for a moment
upon the doorstep and watching the sun sink slowly under the
horizon in a spreading flush of red and gold.

The weeks went by and the baby, Raju, grew. Padma grew,
too, her whole being rounding and softening with the warm
juices that the baby had started flowing within her. She radiated
an aura of protective tenderness—not only the glow of one who
loves but also a sense of possession. It was as if she were surprised to have received such a gift, but now that it was hers, she
would nurture it jealously and claim it for her very own.

I would find her seated on the doorstep of their room, her
neck curved over the baby at her breast and her face flushed with
the ecstasy of his sucking. She seemed almost oblivious of the
rest of us—Shanti, Ganesh, Ram Dulare, myself—moving with
her child in a kind of self-enclosed trance, and we would clumsily
trip around her, feeling like unwanted intruders. I came almost
every day, entranced with her dramatic transformation and hoping always for a chance to speak to Ganesh. He hovered in the

background, bowing politely when I caught his eye, but finding an errand to attend to as soon as I tried to approach him. I could see the lights gathering in his eyes as he watched Padma nurse and move about with the baby; I saw him touch her with his eyes, breathe from her the inner glow that shone from her moist brown skin. Mrs. Chakravorty even remarked to me one day, "You know, if that child weren't so dark, you could almost say that she was good looking."

"She's quite gorgeous as she is," I retorted musingly, admitting to myself for the first time that I was not a little jealous of Ganesh's recognition of her awakening beauty. Ganesh's desire for Padma could almost be felt in the air, and only the preoccupied Padma was unaware of it. Shanti was casting sidelong looks at her brother, and Ram Dulare was shaking his head with scorn and resignation at his son's infatuation. But Ganesh kept out of everyone's way, watching Padma from the sidelines, as if to catch the way she looked from every angle. His growing love for her radiated out towards her like a warming libation, and like the sun upon a new flower, it helped her to grow.

I was jealous. I tried to suppress it, telling myself I was a married woman with no thought of falling in love with an Indian servant boy, but I could not. I tried to stay away, but I could not seem to do that either. Ganesh and I—I was now more certain than ever—shared something that I shared with nobody else in the world, not even David. And although I was not sure what it was we did share, I knew somehow that it was something crucial. I longed for him—I could not help myself. Perhaps it was only an infatuation, but all I could think about was Ganesh. And the more I pursued him, the more he stayed away from me.

The shrewd Mrs. Chakravorty caught me by the arm one evening and remarked, "Your time is very valuable, my dear, isn't it?"

I looked at her questioningly, afraid of a trap, and she went on, "That Padma is doing very well with her baby, isn't it?" She waited for a response, watching my face closely, "You need not keep coming, you know. Nobody is paying you to do this."

She had me, but I shook my head at her noncommittally, thinking only of where Ganesh might be at that moment. I felt continually agitated during this time, always wanting to be where I wasn't, calm only in the presence of Ganesh, even though he said not a word to me. Somehow, this quest to discover what it was we had both seen had become a desire for Ganesh himself. Nothing seemed to matter but being near him—that was all I wanted, and to me that felt like everything.

David watched my growing preoccupation with mystified concern. I tried to be as natural as possible when I was with him, but I was not very successful, and he saw through my guises immediately. He kept asking me what was wrong, and half of me wanted to come out with everything—from the white vision in the corner to this incredible infatuation with Ganesh—but I always held myself back just at the point of telling him. I had gotten in too deeply by this time; there was too much at stake, too much danger I was afraid I could not cope with. What if he could not understand? What if he made light of the whole matter or tossed off what I thought I had seen as simply the effect of fatigue or, worse still, was too afraid to confront the situation at all? Our marriage was still young; there had not yet been time enough to test the strength of its links. If I discovered now that David either could not or would not understand, then a part of me would have to be closed to him forever. That I could not face. Not yet. First I had to somehow find my peace with Ganesh.

It was the end of a long day, and I sat listlessly in an armchair with an unread book on my lap and the overhead fan squeaking monotonously. The flies buzzed around me, annoying me, and Jagdish pestered me with an obsequious whine about dinner, and the humidity made my hair feel like rubber. I was bored, inert, and morose. David had left the house in the morning without speaking a word to me, and I had watched him go, feeling angry and guilty. In the afternoon Mrs. Chakravorty had met me at the market and had gossiped on and on about how Padma was finally beginning to notice Ganesh's attentions, and wouldn't you know it, she was falling right back in love with him! Mrs. Chakravorty had clapped her hands with vicarious glee, not missing, I am sure, my involuntary wince. Even when I tried to concentrate on my vegetables, she followed me, talking on about how Ram Dulare was furious that first Rudra and then Ganesh could be trapped by a girl who was nothing but a witch. When I conscientiously kept my face straight, she rhapsodized on, "And the most amusing thing is to see Ganesh falling all over himself like a lovesick puppy now that Padma has begun to notice him."

Busybody! I thought, picking up two eggplants and a fat head of cabbage, tumbling them into my shopping bag and paying the vegetable *walla* the outrageous price he demanded for them. I walked straight ahead through the market ignoring her babble as best I could.

David returned from the Institute in the evening and found me still sitting disconsolately in the armchair. He threw a worried glance towards me and said as lightly as he could, "Feeling better?" The tears rose into my throat immediately. It was useless to even try and pretend.

"What is it?" he demanded, crouching down beside me. "What the hell is it?" His voice was sharp and urgent.

I shook my head and turned away, helpless and cold. He exhaled angrily, like a horse, I thought, and spit out between tightly closed teeth:

"You've been acting like a spoiled society matron lately. First you play the role of the great white benefactor, getting your nice white hands dirty on the poor oppressed, and then when you've really managed to help someone, you take it as a personal triumph and can't leave her the hell alone!"

I looked up, shocked. "Sure," he continued, talking faster and faster, "poor Padma has finally made it, and maybe you even helped her make it, but now leave her alone! Stop butting into her life, and quit this self-righteous crowing! She can make it herself, baby, and she doesn't need you anymore. Damn it, you're making a fool of yourself, and you're driving me crazy!" His hands were clenched and there was hurt fury in his eyes. Oh, that was what he had been thinking! Oh!

"No, no, no," I cried, finally breaking down and running into the bathroom for a tissue.

"No, no, no, what?" David mimicked. "Jesus Christ!"

I sobbed helplessly into the towel and came out a few moments later, walking right by him without a word and out the back door. My face felt swollen and my throat constricted. I took the path that ran along the canal and into the fields. The bird flocks were chattering in long V's across the sky, and the water buffalo were being led into the water for their evening soak. I stepped carelessly around mounds of buffalo dung, stubbing my toes in the pitted ditches of the path and getting scratched by wild brambles growing alongside. The herder children stopped and stared at me as I passed them, giggling into their hands and watching me with huge eyes. I brushed right past them, hardly noticing them and sobbing openly. Dark, hulking water buffalo lowered themselves slowly into the canal, their heads and curled horns showing ecstatic above the water while the children swatted switches, clucking their herding calls to get them into the water.

The tang of the fields entered my head and began to clear it, causing my nose to run, and with a renewed rush of misery I stumbled on, past the proximity of the villages and out into the open fields where only the bending heads of the ripening grain moved under the sky. The birds jabbered above, and the bugs crawled below, but on my middle level, I was alone. The sun was moving downwards through misty clouds, and as it lowered I felt a chill breeze stir through the air. I shivered a moment and then heard an ominous rustle coming from the wheat grasses. Snakes! I wondered, immediately realizing that snakes had not been found in these fields for years. But still I lifted my hem off the ground and looked apprehensively for a slithering black snake in the grass. All went still, then another rustle, and a sigh.

My heart stopped. Somebody was there. A soft laugh and the grasses moved, not by the wind. I heard hoarse breathing and an urgent voice whispering, "Come, my love, come." A baby cried and stopped, and the grasses moved again, sighing and breathing mingling with the rustle of the green stalks. Wheezing breaths in regular rhythm rose and fell, and the husky voice of a woman moaned and cried, "Ganesh."

Everything inside me contracted, and my skin went cold. The blood rushed to my head and I was rooted to the spot, desperate to move but unable to. I swallowed hard, my throat dry and rasping, and turned around on the path, wishing I could disappear without making a sound. The first few steps were an agony of immobility, but at a certain distance from the lovers I gathered momentum and bolted into a run. I ran as if my life depended on not being caught. I tripped over ruts and lost my sandals and picked them up in my hand, cutting my toes on the rocks as I tore madly by the herding children. I ran until my heart spread all over my body, pulsing its muscles, filled with lifeblood, into every swelling crevice. I stopped for a moment at the edge of the grazing meadow and then ran first in the direction of home and then changed course in the middle and zigzagged instead to Chakravorty's house. I couldn't see David yet. Chakravorty wouldn't ask questions, he would just let me calm down. And running on, faltering and tripping, I arrived, heaving and red, to Chakravorty's house and ran up the back steps to the kitchen where I flung myself through the door.

The kitchen was steaming with the dinner cooking on the stove, and Ram Dulare stood with his back to the pots, facing

Mrs. Chakravorty with a wooden spoon dangling from his hand. Mrs. Chakravorty shook her fist angrily at him, berating him in rapid-fire Hindi. "They were in the cupboard in a little tin box, and now they are not there!"

Ram Dulare hung his head, but said nothing.

"Answer me, you fool!" she shouted, "Did you take those toffees, tell me!" The veins were bulging at her forehead, and her expression was livid with rage. She turned to me without even greeting me, and shaking her hand towards Ram Dulare, protested, "This man has stolen the toffees that I brought back from Calcutta especially for the feast of Krishna, and he will not confess that he has done it!"

Ram Dulare faced towards me and spoke for the first time since the accusation. *"Mem sahib,"* he began, the ends of his apron untying and hanging loose behind him, "I would not take her toffees."

"A rogue he is!" Mrs. Chakravorty screamed, "a liar and a rogue!"

Ram Dulare straightened and turned to her with stiff pride. "I do not lie," he said. His face went blank and hung for a moment, and then he went back to chopping the onion on the chopping board. Mrs. Chakravorty came to me, pumping her arms against her sides in exasperation and presenting a stream of evidence for me to make a judgment on. I stood between them, helpless and miserable.

Suddenly, Ram Dulare put down his knife and began to speak. Clearing his throat, he declared, "I am a poor man, not a rich man." He looked at each of us from the depths of his gray-filmed eyes, his mouth fixed in a line. "God made me a poor man—a poor man eats poor man's food. If my God wanted me to eat rich man's food, he would have made me a rich man." He swallowed the saliva that had gathered in his mouth and looked sternly, like a grandfather, at each of us. With slow patience he drawled on, "A poor man eats *gram, chappatti, dhal*—not toffees."

Turning back to the chopping board, he continued to chop
the onions. The air outside turned suddenly chill, and a gray
wind pulled at the open back door and slammed it hard against
the house. Ram Dulare and I both reached for the door to shut
it, and I saw that dark rain clouds had gathered overhead and
were whipping the air into the start of a monsoon storm. With a
pang, I thought of Padma and Ganesh out there in the fields
with no shelter, but I let Ram Dulare close the door and shut the
three of us into the steamy kitchen.

Mrs. Chakravorty was still fuming, preparing her next onslaught at the hapless Ram Dulare and entreating me to stay and
hear her case against him. I began to protest, wishing only to be
gone from this scene, when there was a splitting shriek of white
lightning followed by an earth-shaking rumble of prolonged
thunder. The room was lit with an unearthly light, and with
shock I beheld a dark form draped in blinding white cloths
seated in the corner. It drew into focus, sharp and dazzlingly
clear—the bald head and heavy-lidded eyes of the man I had seen
at Padma's delivery was staring at me from the corner of Mrs.
Chakravorty's kitchen.

I started to scream, but a long, crashing roll of thunder
drowned out the sound of my own voice. At that moment, there,
at the top of my breath, a sudden, flooding release of peace rolled
through my whole body like the cataclysmic thunder in the sky.
The rains poured down, the earth outside the kitchen pelted to
wetness, while my own pulse throbbed, like the pelting rain, to a
calm stillness; and there, from that calm stillness, I looked
straight at Death.

He sat in the corner of that room, just as he sat in the corner
of every room. It had been Death that Ganesh had seen in the
ward of the hospital beside his dead brother, and it had been
Death who had sat in the corner of the room where Rudra's
child was born.

Mrs. Chakravorty came up behind me and tried to lead me out

of the kitchen; Ram Dulare had gone back to his pots, stirring the steaming rice with his wooden spoon. I stood riveted, not ready to move.

Mrs. Chakravorty tugged at me, still throwing angry glances at Ram Dulare, and ordered him to prepare a pot of tea for us.

"No," I said weakly, trying to brush her aside and seeing, for the first time, what it meant to be half dead though alive—like Mrs. Chakravorty. Inside her were pockets of deadness, like bits of dry desert where nothing could live. They were the lies, the blinders, the mediocrities, the closed doors of her being, but I knew suddenly, seeing Death, that though we would all die, *this* was our chance to live. It was all we had!

Chakravorty blew noisily into the house, streaming with water and stamping the rain from his feet as he lurched and snorted through the hall and into the kitchen. He raised his eyebrows in greeting when he saw me, but his wife complained, "Do you know this fellow has taken my toffees, and then he is lying to me about it and . . ." Chakravorty ignored her, and came over to me, putting a benign, but wet hand on my head and chuckling a warm "good evening," pleased to find me in his kitchen on such a night. With a sudden, wild-eyed lurch, I slipped out from under him and made towards the door, knowing that I had to get home to David right away.

"Where are you going?" Chakravorty shouted after me, trying to clutch my arm as I pulled open the door and jumped out into the downpour.

"I'm going home!" I called back, half choking and half shouting, already thoroughly drenched by the onslaught of the torrent. At the bottom step I kicked off my muddy sandals, and leaving them where they fell I ran, barefoot, through the hissing puddles, laughing! My braid dripped streams down my back, and my toes sank deep into the squishing mud, which tried unsuccessfully to trap my flying feet. Leaping buoyantly across soggy ditches, I laughed out loud, my eyes dripping tears of rain and

gratitude, and raced through splashing puddles and mud-soaked
grass towards David. I was alive! Death had shown himself to
me, and seeing him, I had seen Life. I knew now the real trag-
edy—it was not Death, but life unlived. And almost breathless
with exhilaration I ran, hopeful and crying, across the streaming
lanes towards home. Near the steps of our house I slipped on a
slick spot in the mud and fell, but picking myself up with a burst
of laughter I dashed, covered with wet and mud, into the house.

The next morning the sun rose dripping with fresh yellow
light, and its rays slanted through the crack in our bedroom window curtains. David turned over in his sleep and gathered me up
into his warm bare arms. I rolled towards him, deliciously letting
him surge into my dream, and he murmured into my ear, nibbling sleepily at it. I murmured back, cradling my body full
length against him and running my toes along his legs.

Outside, the morning sweepers were raking across the brick
paths with their brooms, and Jagdish was arguing with the milk
walla as he came shuffling to work up the back stairs. The birds
splashed in the puddles, warbling wetly to each other, fresh and
morning clear.

I could picture Ram Dulare soaking his gray head in the tap
and then putting on his pointed white cap before going to work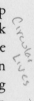
in the Chakravorty's kitchen. He would do his duty today as he
had done all his life. Padma would be curled warmly on a rag on
the floor, the baby Raju to her breast, and a dream of moving
again into the quarters behind Venkataraman's house playing in
her head. This time it would be with Ganesh, though, who was
probably tramping to work, following the same path to the Venkataraman's that Rudra had followed before him.

And Shanti. Shanti would have already tiptoed around the
yoga-figure of Chakravorty to pluck clandestinely at Mrs. Chakravorty's jasmine bush for blossoms, which she would use with
her sacred water and grains of rice to perform a *puja* at her tiny

altar made of mud and river stones, to pray to her God to bring her a husband.

I breathed out and stretched like a cat, pulling myself closer to David and weaving my legs tightly through his, sinking down into the last moments of sweet morning sleep before rising again to the new day.

PART TWO

HEAVEN ABOVE:

The Musicians

"...O master poet, I have sat down at thy feet.
Only let me make my life simple and straight,
Like a flute of reed
                        for thee to fill with music."

GITANJALI, Rabindranath Tagore

I ĀLĀP

The Journey

EVEN AT THAT TIME OF NIGHT the Grand Trunk Road was crowded. We crossed the spur-line railroad and turned onto the Grand Trunk Road in our jeep, joining the nighttime stream of men and animals, bullock carts and pony *tongas*, and flowed along with them upon the hump-backed thoroughfare.

Caravans of carts, laden with hay and headed for the morning market in the city, creaked slowly ahead of us. Lanterns swinging from their undersides lit pinpoints of light against the black night, and we could make out family groups huddled about road-side fires for the night. Alongside us, solitary walkers pressed on towards their destinations, their belongings tied into cloth bundles on their heads and their calf muscles stringy under their sagging *dhotis*. They walked with eyes straight ahead of them, like the patient bullocks plodding alongside them. Mangy dogs skulked through the crowds with sharp eyes, desperate and ready to fight.

As we bumped along slowly behind the swaying bullock carts I tried to pick out landmarks on this road I thought I knew so well. But in the dark the road was transformed, unfamiliar. I could not tell how wide it was or how far we had gone or how far we had still to go before coming to the first crossroads. Except for the small points of light made by roadside fires and the

swinging lanterns, I could see nothing beyond the semicircle of
light made by our headlamps. The road was a strange one at this
time of night; it was as unknown to me as the place towards
which it was leading.

We were setting out late on this night of the winter solstice at
the new moon to a ceremony of classical Indian music that was
to last all night. It was taking place at a village on the banks of
the Ganges, in the ancient temple of the Shivalingam. This full
night of music was to be a *puja,* a prayer to Lord Shiva whose
stone symbol, the lingam, has stood on this spot since the Lord
Brahma placed it there after creating the universe. The *puja* was
to end at dawn with a purifying bath in the holy Ganges, and,
we were told, one returned home transformed—newly born.

I must admit I was skeptical. Perhaps it would be more truth-
ful to say I was afraid, but I agreed, all the same, to go. After all,
I loved Indian classical music even though I hardly understood
it; and how delicious it was to start out at midnight, in the perfect darkness of the new moon, for an unknown celebration at an
unknown destination!

It was Mira and Vikram, our good friends, who persuaded
David and me to accompany them on this midnight adventure.
They reassured us that this *puja* has taken place every year on the
night of the winter solstice since, most likely, the beginning of
the universe. They knew the place well, they said, and were so
earnest about our coming along that we could hardly refuse to
go. Mira had said to me, "I think that you can really know our
India. And I promise you that to know our India will mean to
know yourself."

I did not understand, and she made no attempt to explain.

"Just come with us. Now you cannot understand, but later
you will come to understand."

And now we were jolted against each other as the jeep
swerved suddenly to avoid hitting a huge sow that snorted stupidly into our path, her piglets squealing behind her. I held my

breath as I heard the frenzied scream of a piglet, but we had only grazed it, and it ran into the shadows after its mother. Our headlamps lit up a yoke of water buffalo tethered to a roadside tree, and they looked up at us with mournful eyes and dry noses caked with straw.

We caught up to the plodding bullock carts and pitched after them at their slow pace. Soon we would come to the turnoff where the crossroads is marked by a debris-strewn jumble of stalls on either side, and there we would take the road to the village. The lamps had all but been extinguished at the junction, and we made several false attempts past the shacks and hovels before finding the correct path through them. Finally, we turned onto the dirt road, leaving the bullock carts to creak slowly off into the darkness of the Grand Trunk Road.

By the headlamps of our jeep we could make out the hazy outlines of trees, which sparsely punctuated the side of the road, and the flat plains which disappeared into darkness on either side. For a while we passed some solitary cyclists—grizzled men making their long way towards the morning market in the city, their cycles spilling with sacks of okra and white radishes. They pedaled with slow, steady strokes, pulling their bicycles along the road, breathing puffs of steam into the cold night air. But soon we left them behind also, and with the last few points of village fires in the distance behind us, we jolted into the darkness of the pitted road before us. Wells of darkness closed behind us. On either side of us stretched the unbroken expanses of the Ganges River plains, which are alternately flooded and dried into powdery brown dust with the seasons. Now, in winter, the earth was crusted over—hard as a stone and as dry—and its pitiful covering of yellowed weed lay sharp upon it. The air above was cold and rasping.

The sky was everywhere. It vaulted the land totally, dipping under and embracing it in every direction. And at night you cannot even tell where the land ends and the sky begins—except for that subtle sense you have of a single, flat dimension giving way suddenly to the infinite points of free space where the stars and the winds moved through layer upon layer of darkness. Underneath this sky, deserted and inconsequential in the night, we followed our road. Moving slowly through the darkness, we followed the space of light marked out for us by the headlamps of our jeep. The darkness pressed against my ears and the pulse throbbed through my body as it does in an underground cavern when the tour guide turns off his lantern and leaves you staring with open eyes into nothing.

When the road began to curve towards the river, Mira, who had been silent, announced quietly that there were only about two kilometers to go before we would reach the outlying hutments of the village. The village lay on a bluff above the Ganges, and in full flood the river came right to the steps of the temple to which we were going. At this season, only four months after the end of the monsoon rains, the Ganges was already beginning to shrink from the torrential ocean of a river that she was during the rains to a maternal chain of loosely woven streams linked together by long islands of white sand. Five more months of dry days still lay ahead to transform her into an endless beach of white sand bordered by a single, precious channel of mud-brown water. And then the monsoon rains would again pour down upon the land in wild sheets of rain, beginning again the inexorable cycle of the seasons. But now it was a comfortable river—neither parched dry nor raging in flood—and as we jolted over the hard mud of the river road we could almost smell how far we were from the present banks. It was too dark to see the river, but I could feel its presence on my skin. The smell of earth washed through my ears as the taste of sky and water seeped into my nostrils.

As we continued carefully along the riverbank road, I searched the night for some sign of human life. The stars crowded out the edge of the land, and the river murmured its ceaseless song; but the reassuring warmth of a human light—a light my own size—I did not see. We continued on, each of us silent to the others. Vikram kept his eyes on the road, and Mira hummed to herself as David and I searched out the windows, as if looking for something that were not there. Suddenly David inhaled sharply and I followed his eyes; that was an animal, wasn't it? Yes, a water buffalo—and another! We were approaching a place! And then there were mud structures—just a few, enough of a mound of humanity to make a small shadow against the earth.

It was a tiny settlement, alone and unprotected in the immense darkness. In the inhuman spaces of these vast plains exposed as perhaps nowhere else on earth, lay this tiny circle of human life. It lay a ways off from the protecting walls of the village.

Probably the huts of the untouchables, I thought. I looked around at Mira, but she was lost in her own thoughts.

The villages in the North Indian plains all huddle into themselves—mounds of mud walls hugging a glint of a pond or a tank; they sit like brown dots in the center of the green circle of their fields. And on the periphery, like outcast members of the same family, lay the compounds of the untouchables. The menial workers of the village lay upon their own bit of earth and were taking their rest, it seemed to me, in the middle of nowhere. But as our jeep approached the tiny compound I realized that although this spot was the middle of nowhere for me, for the old man who lay asleep upon the charpoy, covered with a tattered cloth, this spot was the center of the world. This was the center of his world; it was his place, the place to which he belonged. And for a moment I shared his place with him. NOW this place is the center of my world, too. And then I moved on.

Our headlamps lit up first one and then another of the mud shelters. A jumble of shrouded bodies lay asleep on *charpoys,* and a few goats and sagging-dugged bitches lay beneath them. Brass vessels gleamed like gold against the dun-colored surroundings, and the remains of a cow-dung fire smoked upon a horseshoe-shaped mud hearth. The lights and motor of the jeep awakened only one small boy, who struggled himself free from the sleeping family swaddled together in layers of tattered cloths and sat up in an instant to blink enormous black eyes into our lights. As we passed the huts and left them in darkness I could still make out his form sitting bolt upright upon the *charpoy,* staring in our direction.

Again, I was back in the night, feeling alone and nostalgic for that bit of humanity we had left behind. I searched the road ahead for some change, but the road continued to offer the same ruts and frozen weed, and traveling on we pitched and jolted through the black night.

At last the darkness broke faintly with smudges of light from occasional dung fires, and as we approached I could make out simple forms and shadows: a well lift, then a wall, and then a temple flag. I wished that Vikram would accelerate, would get as quickly as possible to where there was light and life; but he came on slowly, knowing that the lanes of a village are tortuous and deceptive. What appeared to be a hodgepodge pattern of paths and alleys was, in fact, a deliberate tradition designed to keep the castes in their proper places and all outsiders confused. And as strangers wandering in at night—and especially in a motor vehicle—we were being regarded with suspicion and mistrust. As we approached, every pair of eyes along the way sized us up and passed the findings imperceptibly along an unseen grapevine. Not a soul moved; not a sound did we hear. But our jeep was regarded attentively as we fumbled through the ruts of the narrow lanes and inched cautiously around the ribby cows that hulked impassively in the alleys. Our progress was slow, and the silence with which we were watched so deep that Vikram did not dare call out for directions. He was apparently confused as to which byroad to take, but he did not admit it to us. The villagers, who all appeared to be sleeping, would know within moments exactly where we had turned up the wrong lane and in precisely whose compound we had gotten stuck. We made a fateful right turn, which took us a long way on a deeply rutted lane between two fields, and we found ourselves finally grounded upon an impasse of tumbled brick and refuse, beyond which stretched an unbroken whitewashed wall. Vikram said nothing, but Mira looked questioningly at him and whispered to him in Gujrati. We were evidently in the wrong place.

Vikram turned to us and said that the only way out by jeep would be to go back through the village, and very likely choose another wrong turning; but since we could hear the river plainly on the other side of the wall, wouldn't it be wiser to leave the jeep and continue on by foot? We could follow the river temples until we reached the temple of the Shivalingam, which would certainly be easier than having to pass by all those silently mocking faces in the village again.

There was nothing to do but agree, and grabbing a flashlight, we stepped out into the cold night air, feeling the ground sharp and uncertain beneath our sandaled feet. I steadied myself against David for a moment, feeling a momentary wave of dizziness; but it passed and I let him pull me up the tumbled rock heap to the long wall.

I clutched my sari and shawl around me, and giggling to each other, we stepped along the wall. Mira said there was an opening in the wall somewhere nearby, and that once we got through to the river it would be easy to find the temple of the Shivalingam. The wall was way above our heads so that we could not see the river, but Vikram thought the temple would be to the left, and although Mira was undecided for a moment, we struck out to the left. The wall continued in an unbroken line for several feet, and then it squared off and became another wall. And that wall angled and became another wall, and wall after wall followed, all without entries! The path was bordered by steep mud walls, and we followed it although it seemed to be leading away from the

river, not towards it. We strained our eyes looking for a chink in
the wall that would let us through to the river, but all we saw
was an occasional opening into a courtyard on the side away from
the river. At each entryway we peered in, but found only a courtyard lit by a smouldering dung fire and a sleeping family who,
we sensed, was watching our every move. Above us, on the tops
of the walls, sprang dozens of monkeys from out of nowhere,
jeering and chattering at us as they watched us fumble helplessly
through the maze that they knew so well. We seemed to be
trapped. There was no way forward and no way back. Mira
looked worried, although she smiled at me reassuringly. We continued on, not knowing what else to do. We resignedly allowed
our feet to carry us along the same path, left foot following right
without sensation, not able to admit that we were lost.

I thought I heard a dull murmur; some sound that was more
than the river, more than the pounding of silence in my ears.
The others heard it too. It seemed to come from behind the wall
on our right, on the side of the river. We looked at each other
without saying a word and moved on quickly. I pressed my body
against the rough mud wall as if to feel for the magic section
that would give way to the touch. Mira ran ahead, and the first
words she spoke during this search were, "Ah, here it is." I
calmed down too quickly, chiding myself for having been so
frightened, and I stepped up to the break in the wall.

The wall broke for a well, and two narrow footpaths on either
side of the well led muddily down to the *ghats* of the river. We
trod carefully over the mud paths and onto the slippery *ghats*.
There was the river again, large and flowing, and above it the
star-cluttered sky. We were out of the maze and back in the immensity of the night. We stood very still and listened past the
sound of the river for the hint of human sound that had come to
us back on the steep-walled path. It was coming from behind us,
so we made our way backwards along the river, down flights of
broken steps and through the debris of tumbled sculpture; along

pathways slippery with moss and around ancient shrines with staring gods, always keeping the river close by us. The murmur of voices was coming closer, and beyond the next set of steps I could make out a long whitewashed wall lit with the faint glow of fire. White flags fluttered from the tops of the walls, and we could feel the presence of other human beings. Drawn irresistibly towards that bit of warm light and life, we pushed on.

2 ASTHĀYĪ
Initiation

THE TEMPLE WAS LARGE. It was larger than any of the others that we had passed on the *ghats,* but it presented to us the same unbroken walls we had confronted on the mazelike path we had taken. Here, however, were voices and light drifting over to us from the other side of the walls. Here was a place that I could touch, a center of human company like an oasis of warmth in the cold night. And although we had still to circumambulate the temple before we found the small entryway, still, my anxiety had lifted. We had finally arrived.

As we stepped through the doorway and into the courtyard, the light and sounds and warmth seemed so natural that I was taken aback. It was as if the dark road to this place had all been an illusion and that, indeed, here was the real world. This was as it ought to be, natural and inevitable—but I still could not quite believe it. I slipped off my sandals and placed them alongside the other neatly paired shoes by the entryway, and padded barefooted into the courtyard behind Mira. Together we walked through the milling groups of people towards the Shivalingam, and we both knelt before it, offering to it the flowers from our hair in obeisance.

The rough stone lingam, the phallic rock that represents the Lord Shiva, stood stout and erect upon the base of its open, yielding *yoni,* its female principal. Upon its virile surface was etched a circling serpent, and the tip of the lingam was garlanded with fresh flowers that dripped with the sacred water of the Ganges. This Shivalingam has dripped with flower offerings and Ganges water ever since the universe began, I thought, and tonight it was I, myself, who was bowing before it. It stood before me with mute power, in the center of this sanctuary, this sacred place at the end of a fearsome road where people have come since the beginning of time. It had been touched by persons of countless generations, and it stood silent witness to all their mysterious presences. Here, on this spot, one was not alone, although only three feet away on the other side of the wall one faced the immensity of the universe in absolute solitude. Through this mass of granite, men could share a piece of the earth with each other and, at least for a little time, not be alone. Here there was light; beyond the wall, the dark night. And I placed my hand on the Shivalingam, feeling the rough granite rub warmth into my cold fingers.

Mira and I both rose and looked around us in the courtyard. David and Vikram had joined a group of men who were standing, starched and immaculate, in flowing outfits of white *kurta*-pyjamas. Their oiled hair shone black above the crisp, white garments, and their white teeth flashed in handsome smiles as they turned and greeted each other. The women were all seated to one side of the courtyard in their multicolored silks, like so many flowering plants upon a spotless white mat. They were resplendent with golden ornaments and shining black plaits, and when Mira brought me over to where they sat, I self-consciously draped the folds of my sari before I sat down on the mat with them. I was introduced to a large, aristocratic lady who *namasted* and turned immediately to Mira to find out who I was. They spoke in Gujrati, and I turned away while they discussed me, looking more closely at the temple courtyard and the milling activity within it. Around the periphery were a number of mea-

ger lean-tos, each a small shelter for one of the *saddhus,* or holy
men, who dwell within the temple and care for the ancient Shivalingam. Several sat in meditation before the openings to their
cells, their eyes closed in concentration and their thighbones
showing translucent through the dark skin of their crossed legs.
Their rounded chests hung with loose, dry skin, and bits of dirty
ochre cloth were knotted about their loins. They sat in meditation, oblivious to the activity about them, absolutely motionless
except for an occasional moving of the lips. One young *saddhu,*
still sleek, his saffron robe still bright, came out of his trance to
swat angrily at a village boy who had ventured too close to him.
But the boy laughed in a high-pitched voice and hopped agilely
out of his reach.

Several village boys played about the outskirts of the crowd,
dashing with shy excitement around the periphery of the courtyard, chasing and teasing each other and tripping heedlessly over
the seated *saddhus.* But I noticed that they were watching, with
the alert eyes of the very young, every movement of the starched
visitors in the center of the courtyard. Their fathers remained in
the shadows, squatting on their haunches and puffing on leaf-
rolled *bidis* and watching the scene through smoke-slitted eyes.
They hardly spoke to each other, but occasionally gave an imper-
ceptible signal to a boy who would come immediately to squat
beside his father, receive a whispered message with a sidewise tilt
of the head, and then run back to play, his expression giving
away nothing.

Bolder were the young men of the village. In their city shirts
they lounged against the well and followed, with veiled glances,
the movements of the upper-class men. Their loud laughter rang
out as a hush began to settle over the gathering, and from one
side appeared several bearers groaning under the weight of the
musicians' platform, which they were carrying to the center of
the courtyard. They set the platform down in front of the Shivalingam, grunting histrionically and flexing their muscles. They

shook out white cloths again and again, and the oil lamps, which burned on every available ledge of the courtyard, sputtered and nearly went out. The platform itself was moved several times also, to make sure that the Shivalingam would be directly centered by it. And each time the white cloths were taken up one by one, shaken, readjusted, smoothed out, and each time the lives of the sputtering flames were seriously threatened. The elders of the ceremony stood by shouting contradictory orders, and the bearers bustled to obey them—until finally the position of the platform satisfied everyone, and the elders sat down again.

I felt comfortable, and lulled by the dim orange light of the oil lamps I relaxed against Mira, smelling the mixed perfumes of earth, incense, and sandal powder and feeling the smooth silk of her sari against my cheek. She smiled at me and I felt grounded, protected. My eyes blurred comfortably out of focus when suddenly I saw, in mystic relief, the contrasts of India within this temple on the banks of the Ganges. Alongside me were the nurtured garden plants of India—the adorned, bathed, and well-fed upper-class people in their starched silks—and squatting in the shadows of the corners were the earth-colored mounds of the village folk—dark skin stretched over protruding bones, eyes colorless, and bodies strung with rags.

My eyes saw it, but I would not see it. I sat up. The village boys were still playing in the corners; their skinny bodies were still fresh, their black eyes still flashed. But those bodies were already working bodies; calf muscles had begun to go stringy and shoulders were starting to hunch over slightly. Covered with ragged shirts and tiny loincloths, they played, mindless of their fathers who stared beyond them to the polished people, the diamonds in the dust. They squatted in the shadows seeing, but unseen. We who were in the light could hardly see their faces; they seemed to blend with the earth, faceless, defenseless. Like the earth they were used to be trodden upon. I wanted to go and be with them, but I felt Mira's eyes upon me. She in her gold-

threaded sari knew what I was seeing, and her eyes grieved with
her hapless burden.

The musicians began to make their appearance from the far
corner of the temple, filing through the gathering with their instruments under their arms. The soloist for this night was to be a
young flutist, a stranger to these parts, and everyone strained forward to see him, approving his tall slender build and his fine-
boned sensitive face. The musicians passed through the gathering, greeting friends with low bows and pressing their palms together in *namaste.* The young flutist stepped lightly ahead, keeping his eyes focused on the flower-garlanded Shivalingam as he
approached it. When he got to the platform he bowed and put
his flute down before the godhead; and tossing a single, yellow
marigold upon the lingam, he intoned his own prayer to the
symbol of the dancing god.

The other musicians came up one by one, still smiling from
their hurried conversations with friends in the gathering. Each
one bowed in turn to the Shivalingam and took his place on the
platform. The platform was just large enough to seat the four
musicians comfortably, and the *tanpura* player settled his long-
necked gourd in the back right corner before climbing onto the
platform himself. He crossed his legs under him and nestled the
gourd of the instrument against his thighs, leaning the long-
stringed neck against his cheek. He plucked at each string in
turn, listening to the vibrations of each tone as he tuned his instrument, twisting large tuning pegs and sounding the strings,
until all the intervals were perfect.

The harmonium player took his place next to him in the back,
and he looked about as he, lively and smiling, unstrapped the
harmonium and fiddled with the buttons to fix the pitch, finding
friendly faces in the crowd to share his good humor. Leaning
over, he checked tones with the *tanpura* player and told a joke at
which he guffawed loudly, but the *tanpura* player merely nodded.
He went back to the harmonium and squeezed it vigorously, pro-

ducing an organlike droning, which faded immediately into a discordant whine as he let go to bow to an elder in the gathering.

The *tabla* player came next with his two drums and a satchel
full of equipment. The flutist waited for him, and they flung
their arms about each other in a strong embrace before climbing
up to their places on the platform. The *tabla* player settled in a
front corner and the flutist sat alongside him in the center of the
platform, his legs crossed under him.

The gathering was now hushed and expectant. The village
boys stopped their game and squatted together in a group beside
their fathers. I looked across the room to David, and our eyes
met above the rest of the company who waited for the music to
begin. A dog whimpered to come in from the other side of the
wall, but a harsh voice discouraged him; and then the courtyard
of the temple was silent. We all waited for the music to start.

The harmonium began, slicing the silence with its whining
drone, and then the *tanpura* sounded. It entered into and joined
the drone, plucking its four tones over and over again, within
and through the perpetual whine of the harmonium. Together
their sound jarred against the ears; I felt the sound rather than
heard it. And as the drone wheezed on, the vibrations were like
the natural sounds of my body, an integral part of the atmosphere, like the sound of one's own breath or the ordinary rustle
of the natural world. So much a part of my consciousness did
they become that they were hardly distinguishable from the silence. The harmonium produced an elusive-toned stream of
sound, which merged its monotonous rhythm with the night,
and it seemed to establish a cosmological arc of music against the
night.

Once the background drone was established, both drone
players settled back and let their eyes close in an easy trance, continuing to pluck the strings and squeeze the harmonium with automatic motions of their fingers. The *tabla* player prepared his
two drums, removing from his cloth satchel a small hammer, a

tin of talcum, and two tightly rolled turbans on which to place
the drums. Each drum sat upon a turban, and he sprinkled the
talcum onto the drumheads, rubbing it in with the heels of his
hands. Bending low over the drums, he listened for the pitch, alternately tapping with his hammer upon the rims and beating
the drumheads with his finger. And when the pitch was right, he
tipped the drum caressingly onto its rolled-turban bed and smiled
towards the flutist and sat up.

The flutist sat tall and reedy upon the white cloths. His face,
gentle and serious, was framed with longish black hair that
curled about his ears, and he was clothed in a flowing silk *kurta*
and loose pyjama pants of unbleached cloth. Facing the gathering, he sat cross-legged, with one bare foot free to beat out a
rhythm against the white cloths on the platform. His simple
bamboo flute lay across his knees, and his fingers rested quietly
upon it. As the arc of the drone instruments continued, he gazed
upwards at the sky crowded with stars and kept his head tilted
back. For a moment his body relaxed completely, slumping into
itself, and then he straightened, the flute across his knees quiv-
ering slightly. As he straightened, the quiet in the courtyard
grew deeper and the waiting company became more expectant;
and in the silence the drones reasserted themselves as sound and
then again merged into the silence of the night.

I waited with held breath for the flutist to pick up his long
flute and give us his first haunting tone, but while the drones
continued, the flutist and his *tabla* player remained impassive and
meditative. I looked around at the others, trying to understand
what part of the ritual this was supposed to represent, but nobody was stirring. At last, from somewhere in the back of the
temple an old man emerged slowly from a doorway in the shadows and hoarsely cleared his throat as he came forward to the
center. He was stooped and he shuffled in slowly, dressed in tight
white leggings and a dark vest buttoned over his long *kurta*. On
his forehead was a large caste mark in Ganges mud—a lingam in

mud upon his forehead, indicating that he was a Brahman and a Shivaite. He made his unhurried way to the platform, inexorably, looking to neither the right nor the left as he walked forward. He bowed low before the Shivalingam and climbed upon the platform knees first, losing himself immediately in the hypnotic moaning of the perpetual drones. He sat there, legs crossed and eyes closed, while the air around hung with anticipation. Nothing moved, all waited, suspended, caught in the timeless motion of the ongoing stillness, the rhythm of the whining drones.

Into this stillness burst a cry of sound. Had it come from this old man? I was not sure. Again, a wail of indefinable sound, and it hung there, firm against the background but elusive to the ear. It ended, and again it was there, stronger and longer. The old man brought it up from his throat and into his mouth and out through open lips. And again, it was gone. Then it sprang up as if from nowhere, bursting from the center of his being and pouring itself out in half tones and microtones, succession upon succession of notes that slid elusively about each other, some round as bubbles, some slithery as a whisper, pouring out from the fount of sound within this old man. His breath ran out and he waited. Suddenly his voice leaped again into a foaming stream of music, gurgling and trilling tones upon tones, mouthing words and tonguing sounds, invoking the gods to bless this night of *puja,* this night of prayer. First he called upon the Lord Shiva, the source of all creation and destruction, whose sacred ground we were on; and then he sang to Mother Ganga, the life-giving, ever-flowing river; and finally to Saraswati, the goddess of music through whom we would all, in the course of this all-night *puja,* awaken the godhead in ourselves and become One with the flow of all things and with the stillness of the All.

The people in the courtyard began to nod and sway with him, softly slapping out the rhythm of his invocation in their laps with the backs of their hands. The old man stretched his arms beseechingly towards the company, acknowledging their participation in his invocation, and opening up his voice he extended, with far-reaching phrases of song, his praise to the gods. His moist black eyes were lit with a deep softness, a gentleness that seemed to imply an acceptance of all things as they were. He smiled, and his smile was a smile of both sorrow and joy—a smile that knew all the ranges of human emotion—and his smile took us all into itself. His voice spun out turn after turn of melody while his stooped body swayed caressingly about his own sound, and finally his invocation trailed away deep down in his throat, and with palms folded together before his forehead he ended his song.

All was still for a moment, and then he raised himself heavily onto his feet, tottering slightly as he did so. The silence was full and round, and then the twang of the drones reasserted themselves and then again blended into the stillness. The old man let himself be helped off the side of the platform, where he took his place amongst the elders of the gathering, solemnly bowing to each one in turn. In the courtyard people sighed and readjusted their positions and smiled greetings to each other across the white mats.

The flutist had heard the invocation with eyes closed and lips slightly parted. He turned to where the old man was seated amongst the elders and he bowed deeply to him; and then turning to the *tanpura* player, he adjusted the peg of a string, and then to the harmonium player, he indicated a slower rhythm. Then he turned to his *tabla* player, and they smiled to each other a secret smile and both looked down to focus their attention upon their instruments. The pitch of the drones had changed ever so slightly, and it clashed subtly in our ears for a moment before the new pitch pervaded the atmosphere and reestablished itself as background. Both musicians waited, their heads bent down in concentration. Almost unnoticed by the company, the flutist lifted his flute to his lips and shifted his body to accommodate his new position, beating out a rhythm against the white cloths with his bare foot.

He started the *raga* alone. A long low note, rich and deepening with each moment until it completed a circle of sound and ended at the point of silence from which it had come. Breath. The low note again, turning in midstream to continue still lower, diverted, like stream water, by a tumble of smooth stones. Breath. Those two tones turned gently about each other, embellishing each other with the microtones of each other, embroidering each other with delicate threads of wine and gold, enwrapping each other in the sound of honey. The flutist stopped, allowing the last turn to hang suspended in the air while he readjusted the reed flute against his lower lip. The *raga* continued with three tones; three tones which hinted that there was more, much more, that would come. Three tones alone which appeared lengthened, and shortened, and embellished, and held on to— three tones in endless disguise to fool us and tickle us into wondering if the multitude of those three tones had any end.

The three tones were played inside out, and the company laughed. The *tabla* player smiled at the trick, and with his head tilted to the side he caressed the drumheads with his palms. I nudged Mira to ask what the joke was, and she whispered to me, distractedly—for she was paying close attention to the music— that the company had to guess from those three notes which *raga* the musicians were playing. And then everyone shouted, having been caught offguard by the flutist producing the three notes in simple, but too rapid succession for them to grasp. But the elders had caught it, and from their corner came their many-voiced confirmation of the *raga's* identity. They jumped up and discussed it with each other, but the flutist and his *tabla* player glanced at each other with smiles of complicity, neither confirming nor rejecting the verdict of the elders. There was a lot of noise in the gathering—groans of appreciation and shouts of laughter and endless discussion—but that seemed to be part of the game, the musicians seemed to be responding to it with warmth. I looked at Mira and she distractedly patted my lap.

The flutist began another phrase of the *ālāp*, the initial section of the *raga* wherein the *raga* notes are displayed. And with this phrase it was apparently clear to everyone that the *raga* was indeed the *raga Yaman,* that the elders had been correct in their prediction. I asked Mira how they knew, and she whispered to me, "Listen to the notes and tell me what the mood makes you think of."

I listened hard, waiting for an image to come into my brain, but all I felt was a kind of musky color with the smell of red earth coming through my consciousness. I described it to her, and she beamed at me.

"Can you also see the sun that sets in the monsoon sky?" she asked.

I closed my eyes and, yes, I could! The sun setting on the plains, the mists rising from the wet, red earth, a sense of peace after a long day of toil—these all went through me. Like the images of a dream, the feelings and colors and shapes and changing movements merged into one another and produced a sense, a picture—a feel of *Yaman.*

And thus, *Yaman* seemed to speak to me through the notes of the *raga. Yaman* was dusk-rose, like the sky long after sunset, and the rose spread and deepened into a robe of blood red, which covered the sky—the sky was *Yaman. Yaman* was the blood-red of night. The night was *Yaman;* and the night flowed through me, like rich wine, deep and red. The night. The heavy musk of the fragrant rose, the bud and the blossom, all were contained in this wine-heavy night.

I was entranced. It was as if I was dreaming while awake. I must have looked excited because Mira put her arm around me, and I asked her, "But, how?"

She tried to explain to me, in whispers, that a *raga* was really a mood, a mood picture painted in sound, and that there were thousands upon thousands of different *ragas,* and nobody could really say what a *raga* was, because each *raga* was slightly different from every other *raga.* But really, they were very simple because all the thousands of *ragas* came from only nine basic scales. Each *raga* was basically nothing but a simple melody in one of those scales, but each melody somehow evoked, with its particular notes and intervals, a time or a place or a god or a dream. Each *raga* was some particular combination of moods and images, emotions and colors, just as each dream one has is totally different in feel from every other dream.

It was hard to understand, but I thought I was beginning to get what she was saying. The flutist was slowly outlining the melody of the *raga Yaman.* Taking one interval at a time, he drew it out, exhibiting the sense and feel of each interval from every possible angle. And as he continued, the *raga* was given over to me in all of its dimensions—not only notes, but moods and pictures and layers upon layers of emotions came through to me, drawing something inside me out towards the surface. The flutist slowly unraveled the tones of the *raga,* and as we in the company were drawn more and more towards him, as our response felt right to him, he began to add dimensions, to heighten the perspective, to make the *raga* grow larger. He would spin out his *ālāp,* the definition of the raga, in his own time, prolonging it until he sensed that his audience was with him and had received an indelible impression of the *raga*'s external structure. For it would be upon that structure that his improvisation would take its flight, and that support had to be deeply imprinted in us as well as himself before it would be capable of holding the weight of his creation.

The flutist's body was centered over his folded leg, and his free foot beat out a slow, irregular rhythm. The *tabla* player sat with his head bent down, his arms hanging loosely over his drums and his body deep in concentration. From time to time a

smile would hover about his lips, as if the *raga,* which was so familiar to him, had taken him by surprise. And then he would
glance around to catch the eye of somebody else who had caught
that unexpected moment, and he would chuckle deep in his
throat, and sink again into his private communion with the *raga.*
Occasionally he would lean over and "puk" a drum as the flutist
reached the end of a phrase, but it was not yet time for him to
enter into the *raga.* The *raga* still needed time to unfold. It still
had to become so integral to the moment that these notes would
become an intrinsic part of the here and the now, under this sky
and in this place. The *raga* had yet to establish itself, just as the
drones had established themselves, as the next layer of the cosmological rainbow, the next context in the order of existence. It
seemed to me that the layers of existence were being presented in
this strange ensemble of instruments as the strata of reality. First
were the drones, like the cosmos itself, merging with the air and
the heavens. And then the *raga.* The structure of the music was
like a universe, containing the sun and all its worlds. The song
of the flute would be like an individual life playing itself out
upon the surface of the other instruments—but where did the
tabla fit in?—that was still to be seen.

The *ālāp* continued, exploring all the dimensions of *Yaman*
until the mood picture had been outlined with the simple tran-
quillity of the solo flute. And then the *tabla* entered! This was
the *asthāyī*—and with the beat of the drums I could feel the
rhythms and changes of the world imposed with startling effect
upon the *raga* melody. Now the flute would no longer be alone;
it would live amongst the rhythms of other men, sharing their
cares and their human necessities. *Yaman* no longer existed in
the sky in some idealized space; he would now have to descend
to the level of the mud-red earth, toiling the toils and dreaming
the dreams of earthly creatures.

The company grew excited as the *tabla* entered, and people

slapped out rhythms on their thighs and wagged their heads back and forth, their eyes closed in concentration. I felt the mounting excitement and tried to beat out the *tabla* rhythm also, but I could not follow it. It seemed to have no recognizable beat at all! It was so complex that it seemed impossible to encompass with the mind. It seemed to imply all the times and changes of the world, its lives and its fixed places, its births and its deaths. All the opposites of existence seemed to be in those *tabla* beats, and all the combinations and recombinations of the parts and pieces of existence with each other. It was too much to take. I was overwhelmed.

Mira waited for a strong beat and then took my hand and tapped out the rhythm in my lap as the *tabla* player produced the beats.

One – two – three – four – five. And then
One – two. Then
One – two – three. Then
One – two – three – four. And then again from the beginning
One – two – three – four – five. And on it continued.

Oh, I began to follow! It was a whole cycle of beats that were repeated over and over, not just one single measure. The *tablas* had their own rhythm, not simply a rhythm to support the solo flute! I was beginning to see; but really it was too much to understand. I tried to stop thinking and to just let the music enter into me, but it was so difficult. Mira pointed out the others in the gathering, and I noticed that people seemed to have let go, they were no longer concentrating hard on the music. They looked softened, almost drugged. I glanced over at David and saw the perplexed look on his face as he tried also to figure out what the music was doing.

Mira leaned over and whispered to me, "Listen to the music but forget that you are listening to music." And she closed her eyes and disappeared into herself. I didn't know how to begin to do that, so I turned my attention away from the music and towards the people in the courtyard.

The scent of sandalwood mixed with river smells and earth wafted to me through the sharp air, and the flickering flames of the oil lamps shone bright against the darkness of the nighttime sky. I wrapped my shawl more tightly, and bit by bit, felt the music and the air flow in through my skin, carrying colors and mingled scents, sounds of the night and the combined presences of all the other people in the temple. Slowly, my body relaxed and I felt my head clear, my muscles go loose. *Yaman* surrounded me with his blood-red robe, and I felt the musk of the night rise within me and unfold like a rose.

The *tablas* beat out a statement. And through the beats the flute slid in, dovetailing the beats and seducing them forward before gliding away from them.

The flute and *tabla* moved together. But then the flute was gone. It skipped behind the drum beats and teased, soft with longing.

The gathering swayed and nodded, moaning with pleasure at the flute's little game. The *tabla* player stretched his neck and rolled his drums towards him. Each musician seemed to be obeying his own rules—the flutist was bound to the notes of his *raga,* and the drummer was bound to the rhythm of his *tal,* or rhythmic cycle—but as the *raga* developed, they seemed to come together periodically with dramatic intensity. "That is the *sam,*" Mira explained, "the drummer's first beat is the *sam.*" After awhile I came to feel in my body when that burst of the first beat was about to come, with a building tension, and with the others I found myself groaning aloud with each *sam.* The elders at the side of the platform wagged their heads happily from side to side at the next *sam* and slapped their hands against their white-clothed thighs. The company shouted and moaned, their heads nodding and their hands thudding softly, with regularity and persistence against their knees. The musicians congratulated each other with sparkling black eyes and continued on.

The flutist rolled out his melody deep and viscous against the sharp attacks of the *tablas.* Using the *tabla* rhythm to support him, he began to let go, to let the music of his song sing out. The *tabla* kept its beats sharp, but modest, outlining the *tal* with little ornamentation. The musicians were giving each other equal space, and the listener could wander from one to the other until he had absorbed the mingled music of the two instruments. Together the musicians traveled on, bringing all of us along with them towards their destination. But where were they going? I still did not know.

I felt we were being initiated, prepared for this journey by a slow, penetrating preparation that would sink deeper and deeper into us until it reached some innermost space where it could expand and then blossom. I felt I was not ready yet. That if this *raga* developed too rapidly it would lose me by getting stuck between two layers somewhere near the surface and spreading thinly. And I wanted to go with them on this journey, I decided. And I wondered if they did not need me, as well, to take the trip. They needed the participation of all of us in order to consummate their marriage with the music; in order that, in the end, the music would speak not by them, but through them.

The flutist was picking up in speed and complexity. He filled up the spaces between each drumbeat with more and more rolling music. He tested his notes and his rhythms with greater daring, and he encouraged his drummer to play upon his beats with greater audacity. But the *tabla* player was still relatively calm and thoughtful. He kept his drumbeats paced and allowed the flutist the greater space in which to explore the ranges of his *raga.* The flute notes, sonorous and then woody, rolled and swayed, the breath of the flutist groaning them out like the sighs of early passion. The spaces of silence between the sound sat, suspended in the air, like royalty, in contrast to the spreading melody that

poured its sweet liquor outwards into all the open spaces. Dissonance broke upon dissonance, dissolving into cadences that
turned over and about before breaking into white foam. The melody rode the wind-waves of midocean where the sea rides the
troughs and the peaks, sliding backwards but moving ever forward, changing continuously but remaining always the same.

The *tabla* continued, still with control and dignity, while the
flute opened up by degrees, slipping deep into the depths of its
own sound and rising with abandon into the air, filling the space
between the depths and the heights with breath, body, and spirit.
The bounds of his *raga*—its notes and its melodies—were incor-
porated firmly into his being. He had made them ours, too, and
now they evaporated into thin air. We were the structure, we
were the instruments! The unleashing process had begun! One
musician began to fly.

His music hovered in the air like a hummingbird on the wing,
with a motion so restless it seemed hardly to move at all, and
there in the air the *tablas* caught onto that same moment and
joined the flutist in flight. They were off! They rode a waft of
melody, diving into it and perching upon it, turning it inside out
and singing its song with full throats. And then they dissolved it
into the agitated air, spilling it with glee, and sped off. The game
was on!

The people in the courtyard stirred with excitement. The elders shook and wagged themselves against each other, and the ladies stretched their legs under their saris. Outside the walls of
the temple a dog bayed. I felt a bubble of anticipation grow inside me and moved closer to Mira, whose body made a place for
me.

The flute tones rose up and up, each tone a spark of warm
light that was extinguished as soon as it struck the cold night air.
The *tablas* gave steady support to the rising flute music, and together the musicians pushed the *raga* higher and higher, straining with their light against the darkness—pushing more and still

a little bit more. A tone-shower sprinkled down in bright sparks, and with a new breath they rose again towards the peak of their own sound—up—and up—and up—and then bursting, bursting through with their light!

The company rose with them, slapping loudly and groaning with approval. And the musicians continued on. Starting way at the top they soared down to their ground, gathering momentum for a long pull upwards, they slid down easily and again sped up, and again down and again up, with a final full-voiced push to the top, where they turned around and around and around again before all breath was spent.

With each new foray of music the *tabla* player came more and more into his own. The *raga* and his *tal* were in his body; he was warm and loose and deeply immersed in the new complexities of rhythm he was creating. He was in continuous motion. His shoulders rolled as the heels of his hands scrubbed into his drums. His elbows lifted up and down by his sides, and his fingers whirred perpetually against the drumheads. Beating against the rims, he struck the stretched drumheads, tapping with the flats of his fingers their black, metallic-sounding dots. The rhythms of the two drums moved against each other, and together they carried the *raga* into the complexities of its simple, single essence.

The flute and the *tablas* moved along together, mingling their melodies and rhythms, supporting each other's flights and closing, by degrees, the space between their music. With each *sam* their modes met and were identical for a moment. And then each took off, separate but inextricably entwined. And with each breath there hung, suspended, a moment of silence—a creative pause—through which the discordant arc of the drones hovered and then melted back into the silence of the night.

As the musicians flew on, they seemed to explore every cranny, every layer of possibility that *Yaman* held. Each phrase they played created a wedge of open space into which the next

phrase could pour. Each note flowed forward, filling the space
that was molded perfectly to it. Each moment became, inevitably,
the next moment, and each note turned gracefully into itself,
transformed by subtle colorations, until it was the next note. It
was as if the musicians could choose any possibility in the whole
universe for the next moment of sound, but they did not have to
make the choice. It was there, inevitable and perfect. The *raga*
seemed not so much to be played by them as it seemed to be
coming through them. It was as if the music already existed in
some idealized space and was coming down to earth, using their
beings as instruments for its execution.

The four musicians sped on and spun out the coursing *raga*
which was entering its final stage, the *ābhog*. They gathered their
forces together and sped through every theme that the *raga* had
offered, making their final statement, gathering together all the
elements, all the parts, all the opposites, all the essences of
Yaman. The speed was miraculous. Like a whirlwind, it gathered
all the separate identities and all the layers of *Yaman* and created
a single, composite image. *Yaman*, the red-robed, rose before us,
red as blood and gentle as pink-hued dusk, blessing us and gathering all the company into himself as the whining arc of the
drones began to dip down towards earth and time. And with a
final surge of creation, the musicians reached the last *sam,* and
Yaman closed on a single note, held softly.

3 ANTARA
The Dance of Shiva

THE WHINING ARC of the *tanpura* and harmonium droned on for a few moments after the last note of the flute and *tabla* had faded, and then they too faded, their arc, too, having slipped back into earth and time. When the last vibration of musical sound ceased, the night and its silence came sweeping in with the wind. And with it, came time.

It was three o'clock in the morning. We were about to enter the second third of the night, the seventh watch of the day. People looked down at their wrist watches, and the seconds and the minutes and the hours—the mental divisions of time—again took their place against the timeless flow within which we had moved during the raga. Two hours had passed since *Yaman* had begun! That seemed impossible. Two hours had passed, but it might have been a moment and it might have been an eternity! I had experienced it as non-time. How strange. The ladies around me giggled, exclaiming at the hour, and the men gravely discussed the merits of the performance amongst themselves. Mira just sighed and lay her shining head with its long, black plait upon my shoulder.

The group of elders seated alongside the platform remained in their positions for a long while, rocking back and forth gently, still immersed in the other time, still hearing and responding to the music in their ears. They emerged from *Yaman* slowly, along with the musicians who were waiting for the music to come to rest, their hands still poised over their instruments. Time re-entered slowly for them, and it was a while before they responded to the sounds of people and movement and flowing river. The cold night air finally reached them, and with their eyes still burning softly, they flung woolen shawls about their heads, hugging themselves tightly in the wide, warm folds.

People rose stiffly to stretch, and I rose with the others, my body aching and numb and inexpressibly weary. I felt the sensation with some shock; I had not been aware of any discomfort during the music. I shook out my limbs and smoothed the creases of my sari, yawning so repletely that I felt something give in my neck. David came to me from the other side of the courtyard, and we stood together without a word, holding onto each other and swaying slightly. The musicians were laying down their instruments; they stepped over them lightly to climb off the platform. They stretched and yawned grand yawns into the air, bowing afterwards to the elders, who watched them with shining eyes.

From behind the elders came two expressionless bearers, carrying brass plates full of *pan* ingredients. The plates held betel nuts and tobacco, perfumed seeds and colored pastes, and a stack of green leaves in which these condiments would be wrapped. The old men pointed the bearers towards the musicians, who accepted the offering eagerly and began to help themselves to their *pan.* Each taking a leaf, they spread some paste into it and sprinkled some combination of the colorful condiments upon it. The *tanpura* player piled his leaf high, and folding the edges over with deft movements of his thumb, he stuffed the whole package into his mouth and began chewing vigorously. The *tabla* player tucked his *pan* neatly into his cheek, for chewing during the remainder of the night. The flutist took only a small handful of betel nuts and popped the woody nuts into his mouth, grinding them between his teeth and sighing deeply.

The elders watched these preparations like anxious mothers. They wrung their hands and smiled with pleasure as each musician helped himself, and then they took their turn at the plates, preparing their *pan* sloppily and tucking the wads into their cheeks began to chew, with bulging cheeks, dreamily. They drifted away into their own corner, and the bearers passed the plates around the courtyard from one group of people to the other, the men first and then the women.

The village men were still hunched in the shadows away from all the movement, and now several rose off their haunches in a single motion and slipped out the entryway into the night. The two or three who remained exchanged some words with the *saddhus,* who had come out of their trances to urinate in the reeds on the other side of the wall. A *bidi* was making its way around the young village men who still stood at the well, and as it passed from one mouth to the other it was reduced almost in half by their deep, long draughts. The younger ones—those who were not curled up in sleep in the shadows of the courtyard— hopped around their brothers for a try at the rapidly disappearing *bidi.* One little one, with a bad foot wrapped in a rag stained with festering pus, hopped about on one leg, leaning against the other boys. A village dog dodged persistently under him, sniffing and licking at the running wound, but he absentmindedly kicked at the dog, intent only on the burning *bidi.* Finally it got around to him, a flattened stub, and he drew deep on it, letting the smoke pour through his nostrils, his face relaxing with total fulfillment.

The bearers marched to the well and chasing away the boys, they lowered the bucket and brought it up spilling with water, which they presented to the elders. The musicians lingered behind, exchanging words with people in the gathering, while the

ladies rustled forward to the well and washed their hands in the
water. Next came the men, waiting for a fresh bucket to be
raised, and then they drank from their hands and gargled deep in
their throats, spitting projectiles of phlegm into the shadowy
corners of the courtyard. The musicians came up and drank
deeply. They soaked their heads in the water, and then wrapped
up again in their shawls before weaving their way back to the
platform through groups of people standing and milling about.
They bowed first to the Shivalingam and then to the elders, who
were back in their places, grinning pulps of red *pan* which oozed
out through missing teeth. After some enthusiastic head shaking
on the part of the elders, the musicians resumed their places on
the platform and took up their instruments, retuning them with
great care.

The discordant twang of the drones started up hesitantly, rose
into a level pitch, and settled into a steady whine. As the drones
started up, the conversations around the courtyard began to peter
out to a murmur, and the village boys went in a noisy group out
the entryway. Some stayed and curled up next to their fathers,
wrapped in greasy mats. A father glanced down at his son and
placed a hand over the boy's tiny rump, looking immediately up
again at the silken figures in the center of the courtyard. Soon the
rustling and the whispers were hushed, and he could look over
the heads again to the musicians; and he closed his eyes as the
whine of the drones asserted itself into the nighttime silence and
became the silence itself.

The harmonium player and *tanpura* player draped themselves
into a half sleep over their instruments, and sighing comfortably,
they let their fingers flick and squeeze out the arc of continuous
rhythm. The flutist sat motionless, his body straight and his eyes
fixed upon the cross of his own legs. His long black hair con-
trasted sharply with his flowing white garments, and the whole
of his body was framed by the granite Shivalingam that stood directly behind him. The *tabla* player tapped the rims of his drums

lightly, listening closely for the correct pitch. The flutist sat on and on, motionless and apparently unaware of the rising expectancy in the courtyard. Many of us gave up waiting, and I relaxed, giving way to half-sleep and leaning restfully against Mira. Fleeting images and changing shapes floated through my mind when, as from a great distance, the first note of the flute spoke, startling and discordant against the drones, and I was brought back to the temple courtyard and the all-night *puja*.

From the first long-drawn notes of the *raga* I was aware of a bluish mist that seemed to drift about me and fill the entire space of the courtyard. It seemed to glisten at first, like ice, but then it settled smokily in the air, like the haze that settles above a village at dusk when the dung fires are burning. The cloud drifted, but then appeared to take up shapes and forms, like the changing images in a dream. It was a midnight constellation, gathering together into a sea-pearl moon. It flew, a winged creature, blue and darting. It became a sea anemone, waving transparent petals through the waves. It rose, rocky and craggy, into a granite mountain, and finally it appeared to be changing into a human shape—a man—a god—a god capriciously dancing!

I was puzzled. Did I really see a godlike man dancing before me or did I not? He seemed at one moment to reach towards me, and at the next moment he was gone, vanished into smoke, leaving no trace. When he was before me my heart swelled, and when he was no longer there I was left with an ache of confused emotion, a double ache, a hurt of joy.

The elders were concentrating closely on the *raga*, and they whispered to each other while staring hard at the flutist for a clue as to which *raga* this could be. They were evidently puzzled, and there was considerable consternation in the courtyard as to which *raga* this could be. Someone whispered, *"Kaunsiranhra hai?"* The *tabla* player seemed to enjoy the consternation, and he smiled to himself with his chin sunk down on his chest and his eyes glancing up now and again to the flutist, who was outlining

the *raga* melody with maddening slowness. On three notes alone
did he remain, moving in every possible configuration upon
these three notes, leaning teasingly towards a new note but always falling back into those same three tones. He let them fall
and sink, like heavy anchors, into the still heavier air around
them.

One old man slapped his knee and called out, *"Chander-
Kauns,"* and people put their heads together, whispering of the
likelihood that this be, indeed, the *raga Chander-Kauns;* but nobody was certain. The tension surrounding these three notes was
growing; they needed to break away from their self-contained circle, they needed to become larger, but the flutist stayed with
them. And just as I began to feel the tension in my body dissi-
pate into indifference, the flute jumped four tones, electrically
bringing us all back into its sway. The company exclaimed with
pleasure and cried, "Ahhh! Ahhh! *Malkauns!"*

The flutist stopped and allowed that electric note to hang in
the air. He smiled a smile of complicity at the gathering. The secret was out; the *raga* was *Malkauns.* We would proceed.

He struck a note that rang ice-blue, like the blue in a crevasse
of snow high on a Himalayan peak. I responded by wrapping my
shawl more securely about me and shivering slightly. The note
grew warmer as he continued, until it was surrounded by currents of vapor, and it dissolved in a puff of steam. Cooling tones
from above appeared and fell downwards, raining into the deep
pool of the original three tones. The flutist climbed immediately
into the whole range of his tones of the *raga,* dipping downwards into the deep, still waters and spinning slowly upwards,
dripping and steaming in the cold night air. He spun out airily
to the top and billowed down, a heavy dark cloud. He allowed
the *raga* to explore all its dimensions, from the most minute
spaces to the wanton reaches of the grand cycle of the melody.
The flutist appeared to be exploring his stage and testing the

ranges of his *raga.* He needed to discover the space he had within which to execute his swift turns and high leaps; he needed to warm up his proper body with long extensions and slow stretches in preparation for the execution of the dance.

The *tabla* player sat impassively over his drums, his blue-veined hands dangling and his head sunk in concentration. The flutist was playing out the *ālāp* with his eyes closed and his body held back slightly, as if to hold back the sweet-tongued *Malkauns,* the dancing god Shiva, from breaking too soon into his whirling dance. Now both men began to straighten, as if the *raga* had vibrated a signal to them, communicating that it was time to begin. Their presence was so intense at that moment that all attention was focused upon them, and as the drones of all space carried us through that moment, the Lord Shiva, unobserved, took on human form from the granite of the Shivalingam and was in position and ready to move when we recognized him.

The *tabla* entered, stepping lightly upon the ground with slapping-soled feet. He paced his rhythm alone and placed each beat separately into its own space. He outlined his *tal.* Shiva remained in the background, allowing the stage to be set with all the accoutrements of the dance before he entered. The *tabla* continued on alone for two cycles before the flutist picked up his instrument, and then both musicians hung suspended for a moment, allowing the silence to throb against the arc of the drones. For a timeless time our surroundings seemed to merge out of focus and then throb back into clarity, surging forward and merging backwards, until all blended into a mist before my eyes.

The granite Shiva seemed to pulsate, its erect form growing and releasing its particles into the cloud-filled air around it. The bright flowers upon its tip and the Ganges water still dripping from its head shone like ornaments of jewels, the anklets of bells that the Lord Shiva wears as he dances out his eternal dance of Life and Death and All Creation. As I watched and listened, the

currents in the courtyard appeared to emanate from the aura of
Shiva's lingam, raying outward and being irresistibly attracted
back towards it.

And into the aura appeared the flute and the *tabla,* the tapping
drums and the honey-toned flute discordant against the twanging
drones. The air was layered with sound, and from out the mist
the sound took on body, and the body took on movement, and
the movement took on rhythm, and the rhythm was the rhythm
of All Rhythm. And from the stillness of movement, from the silence of sound, the Lord Shiva emerged and danced.

He stood on his right leg, and his left leg was lifted and bent
across his standing leg. Above his upper torso were two sets of
arms, which moved independently, each palm at each moment
facing one of the four corners of the universe. His face expressed
sweetness and ineffability, holding in itself the open, creative
pause between all breaths. In a moment every variation of all
movement in the cosmos passed through it, but not for an instant did it lose its stillness.

The dancing Shiva stamped and threw his torso forward as the
musicians reached their first *sam.* The company gasped. His
waves of energy pulsed in all directions and gathered us inexorably into his dance. His feet stamped against the ground and
caused the earth to rumble with thunder. His rolling hips
churned the oceans into milk-white froth. His four arms and his
head and his neck and his upper torso spun in and out of combinations and recombinations, changing with each instant the pattern of the whole.

I breathed in sharply and heard around me low moans of deep
excitement as the company was drawn into the movement of the
dancing god. I twitched, longing to move into the dance; the
musicians acknowledged the response and swayed forward with
pleasure, incorporating me into the fullness of the dance.

They invoked Shiva with breathless sobs of microtonal notes,
twirling and slipping about the *raga* melody, but he remained in

the background, slapping his feet in their time. Again they climbed the rungs of the melody, while Shiva's feet thrummed softly against the ground, tripping through its spaces and floating upon its contours, reaching into the grounded shadows below as the dancing god moved with them, tracing with his body the configurations of their music.

The music entered my body. It came in through my pores, through my eyes, and through my ears; I swallowed it and felt it churn in my stomach. My skin prickled with it and my thighs trembled from it. My blood responded to the thunder of the earth and flowed with it.

Towards the earth the dancing god stretched his body. His legs and his groin were pressed down towards the earth, and his torso swung in circles about his hips. The flute tones followed him, laying deep and sonorous against the surface of the earth. Shiva rounded his four arms close to his body and moved them slowly and simply, his palms facing each other as he traced circles within circles and brought all motion home to himself. He rose and straightened with the rising of the *raga*'s melody, his circles sharpening into lines and angles, the sustained movement of his dance beginning to flick outwards, the rays of momentum spreading out from every point of his body. His arms and legs pulsed more and more strongly with the beats of the *raga*. His center was grounded—grounded in the earth—but the dancing god was free—free to fly! And as the music took its flight from the confines of the *raga*'s structure, the Lord Shiva danced faster and faster about his own center, stretching, whirling, stamping, kicking—joining it and teasing it, swelling with it and moving ahead of it—dancing faster towards the light, and faster.

The *raga* coursed through the musicians, and a deep chested roar of laughter—that glorious HAH!—was coming from their music. The Lord Shiva laughed ineffably, his body whirring behind them. Whirring as he leapt and flung his arms towards every corner of the cosmos, he created a new sound; a sound that encompassed the sound of all the instruments, but was more than the sum of their sounds because it was their whole sound. In this sound, in this dancing *raga,* was All Sound. It was the sound of the monsoon rains and the shimmering stillness of the sun-baked deserts. It was the song of joy and it was the wail of grief. It was the wet howl of birth and the dry rattle of dying. It was the sublime murmur of peace and the jagged screech of violence; it held the tick of the moment and it held the silence of eternity.

And the Lord Shiva gathered into his four arms every opposite in the history of the world—that which has already been and that which is still to come. In his whirling dance he embraced all. As his feet stamping, flew, and his arms reaching, flung, all parts of his being danced along with him. Every particle changed at every moment, crossing and interacting with every other particle. His dance had no beginning and his dance had no end. It whirred through the perpetual NOW, moving and changing at every moment. And his dance, always changing, always different, stayed perpetually the same.

The music and the dance searched and scoured my soul. All my narrow corners and ridged surfaces were swept clean with the bird-wing fingertips of the music. The distinct, piercing strikes of the thundering drums dug deep, beating into unexplored regions, clearing corners and hollows for the sweet liquor of the flute's tongue to lick wet sensation upon the chiseled ridges of my soul.

The rhythm that the Lord Shiva stamped out as he danced was that whirring stillness within which all rhythms pulsate. Each rhythm followed the same inexorable pattern: beginning with an impulse, it swelled to a peak and declined gradually like an ocean wave. The beat of a heart, the swell of passion, the span of a life, the explosion and erosion of a mountain—they each follow the same pattern, each in its own scale of time, each at its own ordered pace.

And in his dance each rhythm moved separately as it mirrored the whole. Each moved by divine necessity within the linked chain of all the other rhythms. And the rhythms together formed an entity including, but separate from, its parts. Together they formed a dancing god whose frantic dance was in perfect balance as it approached the point of total stillness.

His four arms extended and turned, reaching with cupped palms into the space around him. His torso twisted and arched as the notes of the *raga* sped about each other, creating new combinations of sound with each breath. The dancer rocked forward from his hips, seductively gyrating, the perspiration streaming from his smooth brown chest. The flute sobbed a triplet of longing over and over again as Shiva rounded his strong arms before him in a perpetually new embrace, his head gliding magically from shoulder to shoulder, and his face wearing the same inscrutable smile it has worn since the beginnings of time. The flute began to shudder, shaken by the pounding of the feet of Shiva. The *tabla* beats embraced the flute tones with steadying walls of rhythm, against which the flute could shudder. The flute tones rose one by one from the depths to the heights, the air shaking with trembling and thunder as they rose, shuddering. On and on they went, the dancing god and the music of the *raga* propelling each other into greater and greater action. The music was drawn more and more into the central nimbus of the seated musicians, and it flowed out to us from the hub of the dance as one single sound. That sound reached into the taproots of existence, the molten ground of life's sources. Lord Shiva moved with it, dancing with deeper and deeper intensity until all the music was swept up by the winds of his movement into the center of his whirring body. And as *Malkauns* reached a point of perfect balance the sound emerged as one divine tone of music. *Malkauns* came to rest, balanced by itself, surrounded by itself, filled with itself, larger than itself, and ended.

4 ĀBHOG
The Golden Flower

THE LAST NOTE OF MALKAUNS hung suspended in the air above us for several moments before anybody stirred. Shaky sighs rolled through the courtyard, and deep exhalations. I kept that last tone deep within myself, not wanting to let it go, not wanting to share it. The elders in the corner were rocking back and forth with their eyes closed and were humming a steady hum that seemed to extend the final note of the *raga,* providing a bridge between the divine sound and the human sound. Several of us caught their sound and hummed along with them, thinning the sound of Lord Shiva's dance down to human proportions. And as the timeless whirr of eternity slowed down through our humming, my eyes opened slowly, and the minutes began ticking in.

The mist had cleared in front of me, and I saw the four musicians seated in bold relief, outlines of white and black, against the granite Shivalingam. The lingam stood utterly still, its flowing arms and legs molded into one perfect organ of creative power. It was a shaped mass of granite, hewn from the earth by the hand of the Lord Brahma, and placed at this spot by the Ganges. I was prepared not to believe the time, and indeed could hardly believe that it was already five in the morning. We were entering the last watch of the night; the night was almost over.

The two bearers crept about the periphery of the courtyard,

filling the oil lamps upon the ledges from a long-spouted brass vessel. The flames flickered for an instant and then burned more brightly, creating half-moons of orange light upon the earthen walls behind them. The bearers reappeared and slunk through the company with steaming goblets of tea—a thick, dark brew mixed with cream and molasses—and I warmed my hands gratefully about my clay cup and drank with greedy gulps although the tea scalded my lips and tongue. The hot tea brought my cold, numb body back to life, and Mira and I both stretched our legs under our saris and waved to David and Vikram. A breeze blew in over the walls from the river and mingled the treacle smell of the tea with the earth-brine fragrance of the river. Mixed with the sound of whispering voices and the flickering of orange flames against the shadowy walls, there was a gentle hum of sensation that seemed to me natural and, in its very naturalness, mysterious.

Nobody had risen, and all the conversations were held in hushed tones. The musicians were still in their places, and they sipped at their goblets of steaming tea without speaking to each other. In the corner the old men murmured amongst themselves and slurped gingerly at their tea. The *saddhus* were curled in sleep upon the ground, having fallen over in their trances, and the village men had all gone. Only a small company was left in the courtyard by the Ganges.

The last *raga* of the night, Mira told me, would be the valedictory Bhairavi, the mother *raga* out of which *Malkauns* had been born. Bhairavi was one of the nine basic scales from which all *ragas* come, and she kept her own identity as the *raga* with which the dawn was welcomed. With her tonight, we were to move from the night into dawn, just as the consort of Shiva, Shakti, moves inexorably towards union with her Lord Shiva.

The musicians were calm and unsmiling as they placed their cups of tea beside them and picked up their instruments. The *tanpura* and harmonium players started automatically to finger

their instruments, filling the courtyard immediately with their
sound. The discordant throb merged again with the atmosphere,
becoming again the arc of the atmosphere. The elders sighed and
leaned against one another; the women tried to keep their heads
from nodding into sleep, and the men swayed sensuously with
the sustained rhythm of the whining drones. The musicians
shifted closer to one another and smiled intimately before they
closed their eyes gently, each moving to his own rhythm. Directly behind them stood the Shivalingam, erect and still, await-
ing the presence of Bhairavi, who was Shakti, to take breath and
create.

The flutist raised his flute to his lips and breathed out the first
tone of the *ālāp*. It was the same single, balanced tone upon
which *Malkauns* had ended. It was a warm tone, golden and
rounded as an untouched sundrop upon the green pad of a lotus
blossom. The tone was played over and over, beating its rays into
me like the warming rays of the morning sun after the dank cold
of the night. And then it glided peacefully on to the next tone of
the *raga,* drifting softly through a dimensionless sky from one
rounded note to the next, spelling out the *ālāp* with tones of soft
white and gold. Bhairavi was like the pure contours of the lotus
bud that floats and glows upon the pads of the lotus pond, await-
ing the warm rays of the morning sun to unfold her, open her
into a perfect blossom.

The *raga* pulsed through me, making my heart pound hard in
my chest. I felt a bubble of anticipation grow inside me. I found
it hard to stay still, but the notes of the *raga* held me down, floating in pure peace above me, drifting way out of my reach. I
wished somehow to be able to climb onto them and ride them
wherever they led, but I was afraid, also. It was too new, too
soon. The golden tone sounded over and over, resounding a
chord within me that was warm and melting, finding its response
in that space where it could potentially unfold and flower. The
pressure of the tone was painful, and I longed for it to cease just

for a moment until I was ready for it. And then the note changed, and I was lifted easily with it into the ether of a dimensionless world, carried upon the wind-stream of music towards the light, as if I were Bhairavi herself floating towards her Lord Shiva.

The flute dug deeper into his scale, urgently imprinting the notes of his *raga* so that he could slough off his structure and fly, untrammeled, into pure creation. Like a snake in spring, he struggled out of his old skin, with the immediacy and breathless haste that also said, "Not yet, not yet. It is not yet time." The *raga* still needed time before taking its flight, but the flutist played with stifled cries, with the urgent desire to take to the wing and pour out his song. His music ached with holding back, his tones cracked with the anguish of anticipation. The notes were filled, filled almost to breaking, but he held back his impulse to soar, controlled each phrase of the *ālāp* with stillness and dignity until that last moment before the entrance of the *tabla*. And then when the drums entered with their first beat he spilled over and took a running leap into the air!

The *asthāyī* had begun! The real game was on! The company groaned and I swallowed hard. The drumbeats and the golden flute honey took to the air together—they flew, they flew! They spilled towards each other, relieved and joyous to be together again. Chasing each other up and down the scale of the *raga,* under and above the rhythm of the *tal,* they teased and laughed, whispered, and roared their communion. The flute poured a melody to the drums, fluting intricate warbles of song through bubbles of churned tumult for the drums to follow; and the *tablas* snatched the song on the upbeat, thumping it back to the flute embellished with its own rhythms. It was a hawk in full flight, throat arched upwards and wings beating upon the currents of air, beating. The flute sighed and trilled upon a waft of sea breeze, approaching and receding with the surf—and then it swooped up and away, turning and teasing upon air currents, never tiring, never resting. But the drummer caught the song and thrummed it back, diving with it through layers of air and sea, whirlpooling it, accreting bulk and girth to the small-beaked song of the flute, adding the power of its deep throat to overwhelm the fluttering melody of the flute-bird. The flute opened its high throat and poured out its passion, filling winds and waves with its rapture—its rounded calls singing and gasping, singing and gasping. And the tabla player watched with shining eyes; his body tilted forward, and he whirred his fingers against the drumheads softly and swiftly, letting the sound grow bigger and bigger, placing strong, single beats into the whirring, spaced closer and closer. He caressed and pounded his drums, perspiration flinging from his wild black hair—and Oh! and Oh! and Oh! The flutist and the drummer burst with their *sam,* rolling and murmuring together, their beats and birdcalls dissolved into one another, and they floated, entwined, towards the next, gentle *sam,* spent, throbbing, exhausted.

The wheel continued to turn, lifting me above the earth and dipping me back towards the earth. I was being carried upon a wheel of infinite spokes, a wheel whose hub was a lotus bud. The bud of the lotus was Bhairavi, it was Shakti, reaching towards her Lord, reaching. With a gasp of longing Bhairavi pulsed and lifted, pulsed and lifted until the bulk of her Lord was before her. Her body touched his, and as he took her into himself, the lotus bud swelled—swelled—it loosed its clasped petals and bloomed! A blossom. A perfect blossom.

The golden flower shone. It effaced the granite which was Shiva. It effaced the lotus bud which was Bhairavi. It contained each, but it was neither. It was both. It was both and it was All. And the lotus blossom turned slowly, its petals loosening and raying endlessly in all directions. Like a wheel of light, it turned, it turned.

The raga had reached the *ābhog.* The music streamed, breathless, through the golden spokes of the lotus blossom. It poured in rays of golden song through me and through the courtyard, spreading outward into the night. The rays turned, unfolding blossom after blossom of budding flower. They touched chords of resonance never touched before, radiating into the molten center of my being. I was struck deep in my aching core with a lightning strike of gold; it dug hotly and turned upon the same spot over and over again, and I felt a sudden wrench, a gasp of searing pain, and within me shuddered an identical lotus blossom. It opened like the golden flower of Bhairavi and turned gently upon itself. I was moving with the music. I was the music.

Within me was everything—everything that there was! Like the hub of the wheel I partook of all the spokes! I was the night and the day; I was the male and the female; I was the subject and the object; I was the heaven and the earth. Within me was all death, and within me was all life. I was the creator and destroyer; I glowed with beauty and was grotesque with ugliness. I was this moment, and I was forever.

I mirrored the universe, I was its microcosm. I *was* the universe. But there was no I; there was no universe. There was simply this moment of Being, and then the next moment of Being. But there were no moments.

There simply was

And as the lotus blossom continued to turn, I was filled with love, filled so radiantly with love that my love brimmed over and spread outward in every direction. It was a wellspring discovered. My love poured out into the temple and embraced the others into myself. It flowed out through the village, scooping up the villagers and feeling their flat, fertile land. It knelt down and worshiped the sharp yellowed weed, its roots and its crown, its life and its death. It rose into the snowy peaks of the Himalayas and blessed the snow and the rain, and it fell earthward with the melting springs and joined the waters of the holy Ganges. And blessing all that there was, I was in turn, blessed. Worshiping, I was worshiped. I felt the universe bow in turn to me, as the first glimmer of the light of dawn began to break through the darkness of the night.

The *ābhog* of Bhairavi embraced the light and the dark in its final statement. It filled the courtyard and it spun a web of golden threads around us all, linking us together with its golden light. It sped on, spreading wider and wider as the flute melody reached towards the source of melody and the drums dug deeper into the pulse of All Rhythm. The two musicians moved towards their divine center but simultaneously spread outward towards the rim of the endlessly turning wheel of the All. And as the *raga* moved towards both poles of its existence, the tension of the very movement in opposite directions pulled the musicians forward. And as the wheel continued its timeless spinning, the last pure tone of the *raga* emerged from it, filling and dissolving into the air. I felt the tone emerge as if from myself; I felt it emerge from the dawn. And with it, and upon it, I rose with the others and drifted into the breaking darkness towards the doorway and out onto the *ghats* of the river. The steps under my bare feet were cold and coated with wet mud. I held onto David's arm to keep from slipping and descended the steps, lifting the hem of my sari out of the wet.

Layers of light were opening at the horizon, and with wonder I watched them grow, feeling pulses of light from my own heart go out towards them. I walked down towards the river, floating through the early morning air.

To my side—from behind me? I heard a hoarse cackle; I turned my head in its direction. There at my side stood a village woman, stooped and toothless and peering into my face with wrinkled curiosity. Glass bangles tinkled on her loose-skinned arm as she threw an edge of her threadbare sari over her head. Her eyes were filmed over with milk-gray cataracts and she put her gaunt face into mine in order to see me better. Behind her came others, treading down the steps of the *ghat* on noiseless feet, their faces taut with suspicion, their bodies emaciated and dry. From the reeds an old crone screeched, her bony knees scraping her ears as she squatted, and I turned away as I heard the soft thud of her bowels hit the earth. The women slipped down to the water, splashing water into their brass vessels from the smooth surface of the early morning river.

I felt dazed. I was overcome with a nausea of emotion. I could not understand. I searched the golden flower within me, pleading with it for an answer. But it had none to give me. In dizziness and confusion I turned to the village women who were slipping into the reeds for their morning toilets; my love and my pain reached out to them, it begged them for something—for what? But they squatted and turned their backs on me, laughing, and making mock of me. I heard a gurgling expulsion of air followed by a coarse cackle of derision, and my heart within me split, devastated.

Clinging to my husband I moved automatically towards the river with the others, and when the space opened before me I stepped, shaky and off balance, into the flowing waters. I gasped with the cold as the water hit my legs with a shock, but I waded deeper in and let the cold water soak me as my head spun wildly around, my eyes achingly trying to follow the circle. The wheel was spinning madly, madly—laughing wildly at me. I tottered at the edge of consciousness, my stomach heaving with nausea. I felt I was a speck being flung towards the rim of a wheel which had no rim, that I would be thrown off or that I would spin forever in this sickening flight—that the spinning would never slow down. And then, suddenly, I knew that the wheel had no rim. *That* was the point! The wheel had no rim that I would ever see. With the others, I was riding that wheel and would never see the end of the spokes. Like the others, I sat in the hub, an ever-raying lotus whose petals could unfold endlessly and in joy towards an ever-receding rim.

That was what I had to learn from the music—that I could never see the whole thing, that I would never understand. To know profoundly that I had to live, and live deeply every moment of my life, but never, never would I understand why.

And with the waters flowing over me on their way to the sea, I watched as the sky flushed with light, and the sun of the new day rose red over the Ganges.